OLD SCHOOL
HOT RODS

REGRET
LANSING, MICH

Alan Mayes

Published by

An Imprint of F+W Publications

700 East State Street • Iola, WI 54990-0001
715-445-2214 • 888-457-2873

Our toll-free number to place an order or obtain
a free catalog is (800) 258-0929.

Library of Congress Catalog Number: 2006922396

ISBN 13-digit: 978-0-89689-245-3

ISBN 10-digit: 0-89689-245-X

Designed by Jamie Griffin

Edited by Tom Collins

Printed in China

Dedication

This book is dedicated to my beautiful wife, Debbie, who endured many days of being ignored while I hammered away at my project.

OLD SCHOOL HOT RODS

Table of Contents

Acknowledgments

It may sound like a cliché, but this book project really is a result of the collaboration and help of many people. More surprisingly, most of them are people whom I didn't know before I started the project. I am appreciative that there are enthusiasts like those who have preserved the old hot rods, the people who have painstakingly restored the cars that needed to be, as well as those who have wisely allowed some other cars to retain their originality. There is a place for both and these wise people know which is which.

The car owners bent over backwards (not literally; many of them are older than I) to meet my needs, arranging to spend whole days with me so I could photograph their gorgeous machines. A few even washed their cars, too. Many didn't, and I shot the photos with a little dust or mud in the usual places.

All of the cars' owners are listed in their respective chapters, so I will not list them all over again. It's obvious I could not have done the book without them, so I am deeply indebted to them all. There were a few who even went beyond the call though, so I'll tell you a little about them.

Bob Merkt and his lovely bride actually delayed their honeymoon by several hours so that I could photograph their car, and then they drove the car several hundred miles on that trip. Johnnie Walker drove his Hemi-powered '32 5-window in from Gunnison, Colorado, to Colorado Springs just for our photo shoot. That's a 330 mile round trip. Obviously, his car is a driver.

My hot rod sleuth and friend in Colorado, fellow writer Roger Jetter, is responsible for finding many of the cars featured here. He put in place a word-of-mouth chain that netted some breathtaking machinery, plus rumors and promises of more to come.

And then there is my Indianapolis connection. Much appreciation goes to John and Dustin Cooper for hosting me for several hours as we looked through the Cluster Busters' memorabilia and to the club in general for allowing me to sit in on one of their meetings and look at their cool old goodies. Thanks, too, go to Roy Caruthers who not only ran me around looking at some great craftsmen's work in Indy, but put me on the trail of some gems that will appear in print later.

The hair-raising '32 roadster ride that John Couch took me on while I was in Michigan is something I'll never forget. I try, but sometimes I wake up screaming anyway. The doctor says time will help, but I'm not sure.

A few folks loaned me pictures to use to illustrate various chapters. I appreciate their generosity in entrusting their valuable photos to a perfect stranger (well, OK, nobody's perfect, but you know what I mean). Those generous gents were Larry Jordon, Warren Longwood, and Albert Drake. Thanks also go to the huge, faceless swap meet known as eBay, whoever you are. Some of the old magazines and photos came from there.

Introduction
– Old School Hot Rods

When editor Brian Earnest and I first discussed this book, I think we may have had different ideas about what the title, *Old School Hot Rods*, would connote. And I think that is because the term "old school" has become so overused recently that it has no clear meaning. However, it is also a very popular term, so universal in its usage that everyone wants to cleave to the old school "whatever," even though few can define it.

The best definition I have ever heard or seen came from artist Wayne Mauro: "Simple and cool; that's old school."

I certainly have no idea what you think old school is but I hope the hot rods in this book meet your approval, even if they don't fit your personal meaning of old school. These are some very significant and wonderful examples of some of the coolest hot rods in the United States, which is the birthplace and home of the coolest hot rods in the world.

My criteria for choosing the cars featured in this book was simple, and I appreciate Brian's willingness to let me follow my instincts with no interference from him or the rest of the Krause staff. Come to think of it, maybe they don't have a clear definition of "old school" either. No wonder they didn't interfere!

Back to *my* criteria. Not just any car that the owner or his first cousin called an "old school hot rod" was going to earn a place in my hot rod book. No siree, Bob.

A hot rod is simple and has no extraneous pieces on it other than maybe a classy emblem or molding or two. A hot rod is motoring at its basic best—a body, a chassis, minimal amenities, and a hot engine. That's it. It doesn't have much else. Most of the cars here don't have radios. Some don't even have tops or fenders.

I also didn't go for the oft-described "period correct" car if it was ugly or faddish. Not all popular styles from over the decades deserve to be preserved or even remembered, other than as a lesson to never be repeated. Classic good looks and taste are timeless. That's why there are no wooden running boards, shag carpets, pink velour interiors, or…well, you get the idea. Every car in this book is period correct with the exception of some added features as nods to safety or drivability, yet most give little hint of when it was actually constructed. Timeless, classy.

The original plan was to have only hot rods that were what I'd call drivers, as opposed to ones that seldom if ever see road service. I deviated from that self-imposed rule on only two cars: the Couch '34 coupe and the Jordon/Hines Golden Nugget. The reason is that both of these cars are so historically significant (and exquisitely restored) that I'm not sure even *I* would drive those cars much if they were mine…and I think every car should be driven! It's not that they are not roadworthy, because they certainly are. The preventing factors have to do with distracted drivers in SUVs talking on their cell phones, reading a newspaper, eating a Whopper and drinking a steaming hot cup of Starbucks' finest blend, all at the same time as they barrel down Michigan's pot hole riddled I-94 at 80 MPH.

Those two '34s are what I call "custom rods," meaning they fit the definition of a hot rod, but they also have an extra element of style, and custom body touches that let them live two lives. They are customs and they are hot rods; they are custom rods. Look at them and see what I mean. They are encyclopedia "custom rods."

In today's vernacular, they might be considered "street rods" because of their high level of finish, but that term did not exist when they were built. One other car in our assortment would probably be considered a street rod by most people, too, and that is Julie Thomas' '46 Ford coupe. Call it that if you want. It's pretty slick, but it's Julie's daily driver. The mods made to the car, especially the vintage Buick Nailhead engine, qualify it as a hot rod for me, so we'll go with that.

I looked for two kinds of cars, both very much alike. I either wanted survivor cars—that is, vintage hot rods built "back in the day,"—or cars built more recently but in such a fashion that someone might look at the car and think that it could have possibly been built 30, 40 or 50 years ago. Lucky for me, with a lot of help I was able to find outstanding examples of both types of cars. One was built in 1936. Two have been in the same families for over 50 years. Some others were built in the 1950s and have been restored. A couple of them were built less than three years ago, but you cannot tell by looking. That's what I was after—cars so traditional that it was impossible to tell by looking when they were actually built. Some of them fooled me, even as I stood inches from them photographing their every detail.

I also set out to find cars that had not had much, if any, magazine exposure. There were a couple of reasons behind that goal. One, I don't think it's fair to the reader to show you cars that have been plastered all over magazines because you've probably already seen those. Two, there are obviously great cars out there that haven't had the exposure (or overexposure) that some other cars have had.

You may also note there are no California cars in this book. Not that there is anything wrong with Cali cars. There are thousands of great hot rods there. But cars from the rest of the country have often been overlooked, quite possibly because most of the mainstream rodding media is based in California. All of the cars in this book reside between Gunnison, Colorado, and Atlanta, Georgia.

The main factor deciding whether or not a hot rod made it into the book was a pretty simple one, and one that only I could ultimately determine. The car had to have *the look*. It's hard to describe, but my best way of knowing when a car has it is simply how I respond to it. There are certain cars that you cannot stop looking at. Every one of the cars in this book had that effect on me. Thankfully, I didn't often see more than one at a time. When I did, I almost had whiplash from looking back and forth. I first saw a few of these rods at the 2005 Detroit Autorama. I spent three days there, covering the event for *Ol' Skool Rodz* magazine. I found myself going back to look at those same cars over and over again…and then again just before I left. And I thought about them for several days after.

All of the hot rods must have been built by people who either had an eye for good proportions and creating the right stance, or they just lucked out. Either way, these cars look just right. When I photographed them, I almost didn't know when to quit. That was the case for a couple of reasons. One, I was afraid I would miss some detail or an opportunity for the perfect picture of what I saw as a perfect car. Secondly, I didn't want to leave the presence of the cars. I loved them so much that I just wanted to stay and spend some more time with them.

As I gathered the material for this book, I came to realize that our world of hot rodding is a very small one. Almost everyone knows someone that another rodder knows, even in different states and different parts of the country. And many of these guys are walking encyclopedias of hot rodding. They know who built various cars that were featured in old magazines or in long-ago shows, who the cars were sold to, where they are now, and everyone who owned them in between.

There is also a huge amount of respect for fellow rod builders, at least for ones who build cars of the caliber we've gathered here. And that respect transcends many differing factors. There are cars here with a monetary worth that would be difficult to assign, simply because of their historical significance. They are probably worth more than the total of *everything* I own, house included. Others are priceless in their owners' eyes for various reasons. Some are daily drivers or close to it. That's how dependable and well-built they are. A couple only have a few miles on them since being restored, yet in their original incarnation they were daily drivers; others have gone well over 100,000 miles since they were built. Paint chips were the rule rather than the exception.

Unfortunately I was unable to include all the cars I wanted for this book. There were a few I just was unable to get to in the time I had due to scheduling conflicts. One or two that I photographed turned out to not be as photogenic as I'd hoped, at least in the setting we chose and with me as the photographer, so they didn't make this volume. I hope to get an opportunity for a rematch with those.

The more I delve into the wonderful world of traditional hot rods, the more cars I hear about. Some day there might be a second volume of this book. I hope so because I had a blast doing it. I hope you like what you see in this one.

—*Alan Mayes*

Historical Perspective

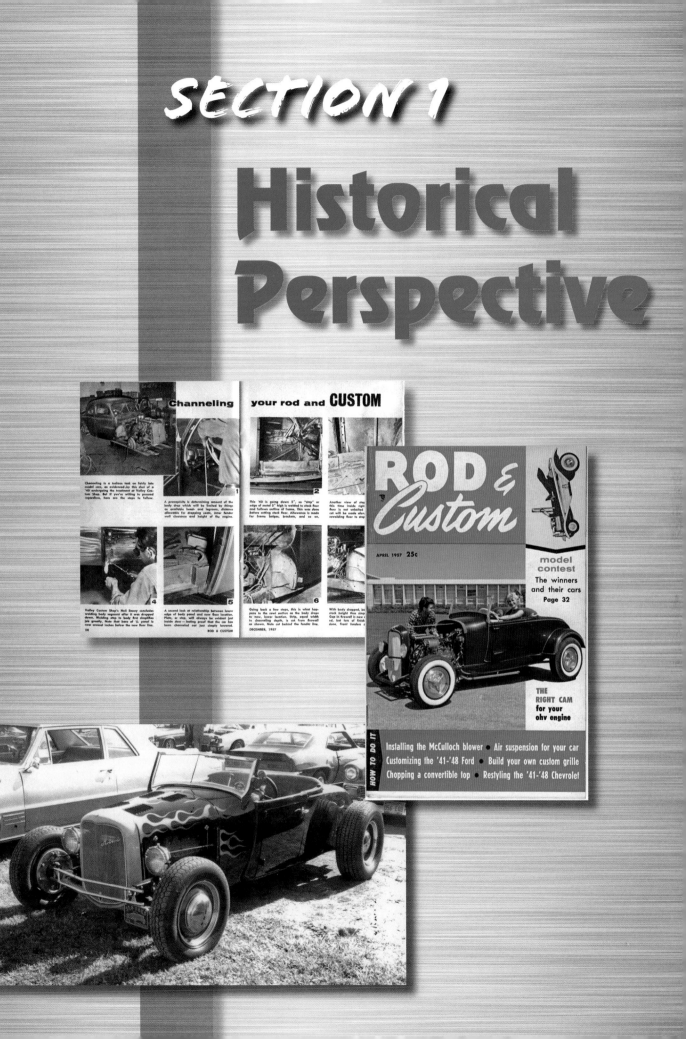

ROD &
Custom

APRIL 1957 **25c**

**model
contest**
The winners
and their cars
Page 32

**THE
RIGHT CAM
for your
ohv engine**

HOW TO DO IT

Installing the McCulloch blower • Air suspension for your car
Customizing the '41-'48 Ford • Build your own custom grille
Chopping a convertible top • Restyling the '41-'48 Chevrolet

CH 1

Roots of Hot Rodding

"Most of what is considered common knowledge about the history of hot rods today had to come from somewhere." That's probably not a direct quote, but it's pretty darned close. Automotive and hot rod author Albert Drake uttered those words, or similar words of wisdom, to me one day in a phone conversation. He is correct in his statement, of course. It's the location of "somewhere" that is in question.

Albert Drake has been researching hot rod history and writing about it for many, many years. Al lived a lot of it too. He maintains that several other

The small magazines were stuffed full of useful hot rod info, like this listing of various makers' camshafts in the July 1957 *Rod & Custom.*

authors have used his books as their source for that information as used in their recently published books and have not credited him for it. He may well be right. I wish he were not.

I think I have all of Al's hot rod books, but I purposely have not read any of them through yet. I didn't want to be guilty of

plagiarizing Al's words, whether intentionally or not. I've read parts of his intros and looked at some of the great pictures, though. I've also read many of his excellent magazine articles over the years. When I finish this book, I'm going to read his books cover to cover.

In the meantime, he loaned me a few of his pictures for this chapter. I'll give credit where it is due. And I'll tell you a little bit about hot rod history from my own point of view. The early hot rods, up through those being

The April 1957 issue of *Rod & Custom* is typical of the small sized magazines devoured by young and old gearheads alike.

Photo courtesy Albert Drake

A '32 Ford doesn't need much to look good. This highboy was photographed in the mid-1940s and belongs to noted engine builder John Ryan.

built in the early 1960s, form the nucleus of what I consider to be old school or traditional hot rods. Even as you look at the hot rods in this book that were built recently, they'll appear much the same as those built in the period between 1935 and 1963. Those years, give or take a couple on each end, were the best years of originally-built hot rods. That's just my opinion, of course.

One man's rodding research

I have probably been reading about hot rods since I was old enough to read much of anything that didn't involve Spot and Fluffy. I was a pretty good reader early in life, so I suppose the time between picking up my first Dick and Jane reader and my first *Motor Trend* or *Popular Mechanics* read wasn't all that long. That would have been around 1956 or 1957, when I was in the first grade. My dad always subscribed to a couple of car magazines and bought some others off the newsstand from time to time. Every once in awhile, one of those general interest car magazines had a feature or two on hot rods.

By the time I was old enough to earn an allowance for washing the dishes or mowing the yard, my allowance went one of two places. It went to J&R Toys and Hobbies in Anderson, Indiana, in exchange for the latest AMT or JoHan model car kit (usually AMT since most of JoHan's cars were Chrysler

products, not as popular in our mostly GM family), or to Johnson's Store in my Daleville hometown.

My best friend, Terry Stotts, and I were completely eaten up with the hot rod and custom car fever. We rode our bikes to Johnson's where he would buy one of the "small pages" magazines like *Car Craft*, *Custom Cars*, or *Rod & Custom*, and I would buy another. We read them from cover to cover, then traded back and forth and read them cover to cover again. Later on I bought *Hot Rod* and *Popular Hot Rodding* and on and on.

While I was in the sixth grade, I discovered the books by Henry Gregor Felsen in our school library. I checked each one out in succession and read every word. When I had gone through the entire limited selection we had on hand, I started over again. *Hot Rod*, *Street Rod*, *Crash Club*, and *Road Rocket*, I read them all.

When I was in high school in the 1960s, my high school library actually carried *Hot Rod*! I knew within a day or two when it was due to come in, so I used to get a library pass from study hall and go down to the library to get the latest issue. If someone else was reading it, I grabbed a seat close to the magazine rack and pretended to read something else, all the time watching the rack with one eye. As soon as the *Hot Rod* was returned, I'd grab it and it was mine for the rest of the period. Sometimes it took two or three successive library trips to get the whole thing read, what with those other guys interfering, but I eventually got it all done.

A Model A roadster runs through the traps on the dry lake bed at Muroc in California.

Photo courtesy Albert Drake

Since those early days, I have probably bought at least one or two editions of every hot rod-related title sold in the US, hundreds of the better ones. I've gone to the hot rod B-movies and watched them on TV. My bookcases have bowed shelves from the weight of all my car, motorcycle, and hot rod books. I'm a voracious reader of that sort of thing and so I suppose my personal "common knowledge" is a compendium of all that I've read over the past 50 years and what I've seen and what I have heard from my equally eaten-up friends. I have cars and hot rods in my blood and at this late date, I suppose I always will. Can't help it, so I might as well write some of it down.

Mark "Briz" Brislawn has owned this Model A roadster over 30 years. It was built in the early 1950s as a track roadster.
Photo courtesy Albert Drake

What's a hot rod?

It's easier to spot a hot rod in a crowd of other cars than it is to define what it is. I know what it's not, though. When Rusty Wallace was still racing, he called his NASCAR Dodge a hot rod on weekends when it was running especially well. It was not a hot rod, though, but a purpose-built race car. John Force does the same thing with his NHRA Funny Car. Same answer.

Based on my above research and more that I have done casually but intently over the past 40 or 50 years, my opinion of what makes a car a hot rod is this: it's an early car that has had its performance increased.

That can be accomplished in one of two ways, or a combination of the two, which is even better. The obvious way to performance enhancement is more power. That comes by either increasing the power output of the existing engine or installing a more powerful engine in its place. The other way to increase performance is to reduce weight. One hundred horsepower in a 2,000-pound car beats 100 in a 2,500-pound car every day, all else being equal. Two hundred horsepower in that same 2,000-pound car is much, much better.

There is a certain cutoff date or look for a hot rod in my mind…and it probably only exists

Stan Ochs is one of those lucky old rod finders we all envy. He located this channeled, full-fendered '32 Ford, had it chopped and added a Chevy V8.
Photo courtesy Albert Drake

in that one dark place, too. Some will disagree with my following nitpicky explanation, but that's OK. Let them write their own books! It's not as simple as the NSRA definition of a street rod either. Their pre-1949 cutoff rule allows pre-1949 restored cars in as well as hot rods and street rods. Sorry, but a restored or original 1936 Packard sedan is not a street rod, nor is it a hot rod. It's a beautiful car, but not a rod.

I think that a '49 Ford could be a hot rod, especially with the hood off, but a '57 Chevy cannot be. No offense against '57 Chevys, but they are just not hot rod material. They are too gaudy and decorated. They can become customs, or great restored cars, or one with a hopped-up engine could be a *hot-rodded* car, but not a hot rod.

The best hot rods are pre-fat fendered cars. Those cars can be lightened up by taking off the fenders and hoods and still look OK. Fat-fendered cars can usually lose the hood without losing face. Pull the fenders off and you're toying with terminal ugliness. Newer cars are even tougher to lighten.

Way back machines

For some reason, most rodding histories seem to begin in the period right after World War II, as though there were some kind of a connection between Hitler's death and the development of man's desire to go faster.

This car may have been a street roadster a year earlier, but by 1954, it was strictly a drag car.
Photo courtesy Albert Drake

Two '36 Fords are typical of customized hot rods touring the streets in the 1950s. The one on the right belongs to Warren Longwell of Denver.
Photo courtesy Warren Longwell

Not all hot rods had V-8 power. This track roadster sports a hopped-up Chevy inline-6 with a Wayne "flow through" aluminum head.
Dave Baumgardner collection

One of the first A-V8 cars (Model A with flathead Ford V8) in Portland, Oregon, belonged to Don "Duck" Collins. It was a daily driver.
Photo courtesy Albert Drake

Really, hot rodding of cars probably started approximately 10 minutes after there were two cars in the same town. Man is competitive by nature and you can be assured that when Melvin found out that Thaddeus' car would go nearly two miles per hour faster than his, he was ready for someone like Vic Edelbrock to step in and up the ante by at least three mph. Vic was a little behind the curve to do ol' Mel any good, but he stepped up to the plate and helped a lot of other guys a little later.

During their 100th Anniversary celebration, Ford Motor Company made a big deal of the fact that Henry Ford had won a race over Alexander Winton in one of his cars 100 years before. It wasn't a stocker, folks. It was Henry's version of an early, very early, hot rod. That was in October 1901, only 10 years after John Lambert screwed together the first US-built car, which was a three-wheeler.

Henry's car had no fenders, no lights, and one seat. It was stripped down so that the meager horsepower available in that little engine had minimal weight to move. Three years later, Ford set a land speed record of just over 91 miles per hour in his famous "999" car. The US automobile industry was barely more than 12 years old and men like Henry Ford were knocking on the door of 100 miles an hour. They were doing some serious hot rodding!

As cars became more common and more available to the average Joe, they slowly but surely replaced the horse and wagon as the common mode of transportation. And the automobile race began to replace the horse race as the outlet for adrenaline- and testosterone-charged young men to prove themselves and the worth of their steeds. The car races took on much the same form as horse races had. They were either run on a straight course as a drag race or timed mile or on oval tracks, which were also used for, you guessed it, horse races.

The earliest race cars were not usually purpose-built vehicles. More often that not, if a person could afford a car, it was only one. If he wanted to go racing, he raced his one car, the same one that he drove to work and to the market and out to Grandma's place on Sunday afternoon. In order to make the car lighter for the race at hand, and to make the available horsepower as effective as possible, the driver would pull off all the extraneous bits like fenders, lights, passenger seats, folding tops, and bumpers. After the races were completed, all that gear was bolted back on the roaring roadster. With the exception of the lights, that other stuff really wasn't necessary for the function of the car, though. Most hot rodders just left all of it off because it saved time and it made the car perform better on the street. It looked cool, too. Except in the rain, but one cannot have everything, can one?

Though Southern California is considered the base camp of hot rodding history, those early efforts were really taking place all over the country. California's advantage was their weather, allowing year-round racing, running cars without tops or fenders more days per year, etc. Still there were hotbeds of racing and hot rodding all over the country.

The automotive industry was pretty centralized, roughly a hundred miles either side of a triangle with Detroit, Indianapolis, and Chicago as its three points. There was major automotive activity in that area, with each of a dozen or more manufacturers trying to outdo the next. Remember we're still considering the period several years before World War II. Within this geographical area were such companies as Chrysler, Ford, Cord, General Motors, Hudson, Nash, Studebaker, Auburn, Stutz, Packard and Duesenberg, plus a few others.

There were specialists in most every brand of car, whether they were dealers or suppliers or racers. Their go-fast efforts trickled out to their fans, racers and dealers nationwide. The parts found their way into customers' cars, too.

Also, by the early 1930s, there had been quite a bit of development and improvement in reliability and power of engines, yet they weren't much different physically from their predecessors. It didn't take the

Service stations were hot rodders hangouts as well as homes of and sponsors for race cars. This one in Denver is no exception.
Photo courtesy Warren Longwell

Bill Roarke's Track-T carries one of the hotter V-8s available in the 1950s and early 1960s, a Studebaker.

go-fast crowd long to figure out that a 1932 Ford Model B four cylinder engine would slide right in the place of a Model A engine and offer more power immediately.

Even since the 1920s, there had been speed equipment manufacturers producing components to make the old four cylinder flathead engined cars go faster. Companies like Roof and Frontenac had made overhead valve conversions for Model Ts that substantially increased available power. Such development had continued through the Model A lifecycle, too. Cyclone, Riley, Forged True and Winfield were just a few of the better-known names in the hot rod world. Additionally, there were hot rod machinists all over the country capable of making their own one-off speed equipment to meet their own unique and particular needs.

Came 1932 and our hot rod world changed forever, albeit slowly. The flathead V-8 introduced in the '32 Fords was a modern marvel in the low priced field. It took a little while for it to realize its potential though. Naturally it provided a lot more power in its stock form than the four-cylinder engine had, but there was a vast amount of speed equipment available for the four bangers that did not yet exist for the new V-8. As a result, a hopped-up Model A was still faster than a stock V-8. The transition didn't take long, though, and within a few years, the V-8 was the

way to go for those rodders wanting to upgrade the power in their A or T.

Note that nearly all this talk about hot rods and speed equipment has centered on the Fords. Why? Because the Fords were the predominant car in the low-priced field. Henry's Model T had put America on wheels, and the Model A was the next step for people with good experience in a Ford. The engines were similar and the home mechanics and hot rodders were familiar with their inner workings and idiosyncrasies.

Through the 1930s, the Ford flathead V-8 continued to be developed and was introduced in more powerful versions. Simultaneously, the Ford cars were getting bigger and heavier, needing more powerful engines to maintain the same or better performance. Then came World War II and the whole automotive thing hit the skids. All eyes and efforts were focused toward the war effort. Automotive production ceased in January 1942 and did not resume until late 1945/early 1946.

More Power! Arrh! Arrh! Arrh!

With the war completed, America was back on track, stronger than ever and hungrier for new cars than ever. Keep in mind, too, that the average car hadn't really changed much *technologically* during

These car club plates from central Indiana in the 1950s are typical of the cast aluminum ones used nationwide. These belong to Bob Drake, Fortville, Indiana.

MODOCKER INDPLS.

Gearboxers FORTVILLE

those years. Part of that was due to the virtual halting of any automotive engineering and development during World War II. New models didn't appear until 1946 (Kaiser-Frazier), 1947 (Studebaker) or even 1949 (Big Three).

Even then, almost all the companies' energy had gone to creating newer, more modern looking bodies, not power trains. The more modern engines and transmissions were still a few years down the line. So, working on a 1953 car wasn't much different than working on a 1939 or even a 1929. Electronics did not yet play a role in automotive design either. Getting a flathead Ford engine from a 1949 car to start and work in a 1932 car was not a big deal.

Unlike today, nearly all cars were of a body and frame design, as opposed to unitized construction. Taking the body off the frame was a relatively easy chore. A few wrenches and a chain hoist, or five buddies, were the only tools needed to accomplish the feat in a couple of hours or less. It wasn't out of the realm of a good mechanic to pull a Model A body off its frame and install it on a Deuce chassis with a few modifications. That swap offered a stiffer, better handling chassis and more power to boot.

With the late 1940s and early to mid-1950s came overhead valve V-8 engines and the rest, as they say, is history. OK, actually this is all history. The OHV V-8s offered out of the box power to hot rodders that they had only imagined before. Cadillac, Buick, Chrysler, and even Studebaker had overhead valve V-8s available in some models by the early 1950s. By 1955, all the makes that still existed had OHV V-8s.

Hot Rod Heaven was born and the headquarters was Detroit, Michigan! There were outposts in every town in America.

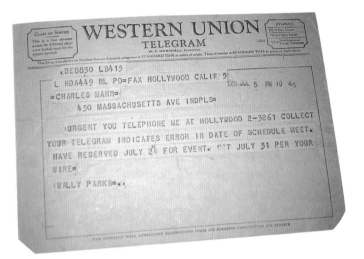

Wally Parks' July 1955 telegram confirming the Cluster Busters drag race date.

The Cluster Busters' photo albums are full of shots of their early Stout Field drags.

A Little Help from My Friends

One of the trends that arose out of the hot rodding movement was the growth of car clubs. Such clubs were often very loosely organized, if at all. They could be as informal as a bunch of guys with matching jackets and/or T-shirts and a club name. Sometimes they were actually better organized and had bylaws in addition to specific rules for the members. Some clubs even had clubhouses, usually a warehouse or small industrial building, where the guys would gather to work on their cars.

One of the advantages to belonging to a club was that there were often members of the club who were very skilled at one aspect of hot rod building or another, while other members had differing skills. Pooling all those skills together made the group as a whole pretty effective at building a hot rod.

Some of those old clubs still exist in one form or another. One of those is the Cluster

Busters in Indianapolis. The Cluster Busters was formed in 1948 and has been in continual operation since then. In addition to a couple of 17-year-old members, the Cluster Busters also has some near-lifelong members in their 80s.

During the formative years of the early 1950s, the Cluster Busters was one of the local clubs across the country that helped

Wally Parks and the fledgling National Hot Rod Association stage organized drag races. Thanks to efforts of Cluster Busters founding member Charlie Mann and those like him, the NHRA became a strong force for safety and consistency in drag racing rules.

Cluster Buster members have done an excellent job in maintaining documentation of

The 1952 NHRA Charter for the Cluster Busters car club, Indianapolis.

The Cluster Busters car club in Indianapolis was begun in 1948.

The Cluster Busters still meet every Tuesday night at their west Indy clubhouse.

Newer car clubs like the Atlanta Road Kings are carrying on the tradition of earlier clubs.

their past. On their clubhouse walls are NHRA Club Charters going back as far as 1950 (and signed by Wally Parks). They also have albums full of early photographs of their drag racing escapades at Indy's Stout Field Dragstrip.

The Cluster Busters currently organize and staff the huge annual James Dean Run in Fairmount, Indiana, Dean's hometown. They maintain a clubhouse that is today used only for meetings and social functions. And they still meet every Tuesday night.

Put That in Writing

Especially during the 1950s, hot rod and custom magazines provided quite a bit of technical instruction to their readers in the hot rod and custom car realms. Many of today's magazines seem to utilize their so-called technical articles as extended advertisements for various companies' bolt-on wares.

Back in the day, those types of articles actually contained useful information with a series of several photographs showing the actual steps of installing a different engine, tunneling a headlight, or degreeing a cam. Early rod magazines were a useful source for technical know-how.

A few current rod magazines still offer useful technical help. Among the best are *Ol' Skool Rodz* and *Rodder's Digest*. Most of the others are paper infomercials.

There's More, but Not Here

At the end of this book, you will find a short list of some of the better books I have encountered regarding early hot rodding, which is the root of traditional or old school hot rods. That is in turn what this book is supposed to be about. Let's look at some old school hot rods.

Useful, step-by-step tech was a staple of early rod magazines.

SECTION 2
Survival of the Fittest

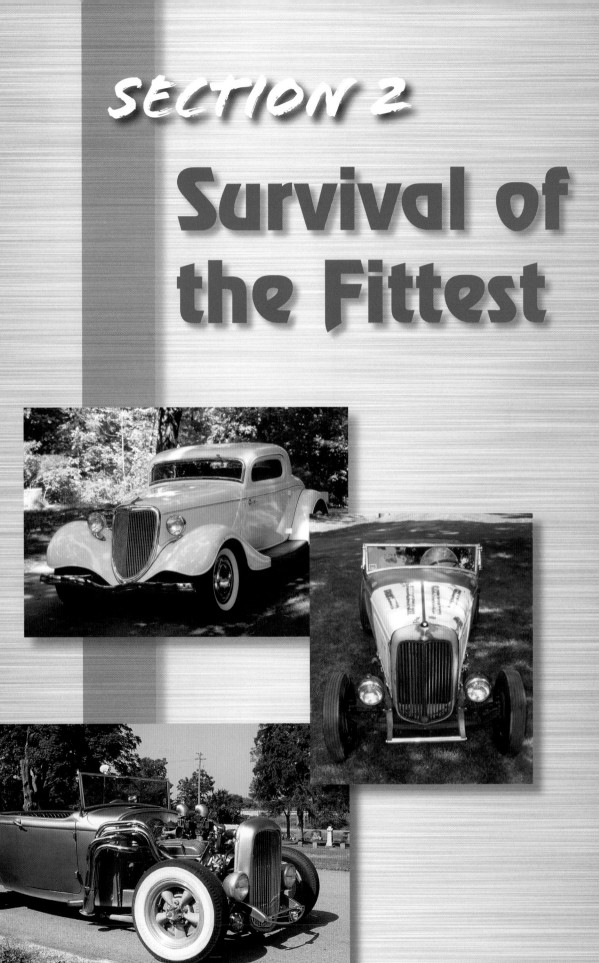

CH 2

Darrel & Linda Helms'
Hot Rod Banger

Some cars are too nice to restore. Darrel Helms' A is one of them.

If you were to look at most of the recent books and magazines about early hot rodding, you might get the impression that hot rods didn't exist prior to the debut of Henry Ford's venerable flathead V-8. After all, the Ford flathead is the usual engine of choice for the average rodder looking for a nostalgic engine to power his traditional rod.

That impression would be extremely wrong. Not only were there hot rods pre-flathead, but there were hot four-cylinder hot rods around that could outrun the new-fangled V-8s for awhile. Decades of racing with various four bangers had allowed their development into

some pretty impressive relative horsepower ranges as compared to the as yet untested and undeveloped V-8s.

Henry Ford raced his cars almost from the very beginning and those cars were all four-cylinder vehicles. Fords were among the most affordable cars on the road in the 1920s and 1930s, so they were plentiful. When people started racing

them, they soon found small companies willing to provide hop-up equipment to make them go faster. Once the very long-in-the-tooth Model T was replaced in 1928 by the Model A, it didn't take long for speed equipment makers to latch onto the new engine and start providing go-fast pieces for it. Even for several years after the flathead V-8 appeared, some potent Model A fours still ruled the roads. The 1932 Ford Model B four cylinder was very similar to the Model A's and benefited from the "research" done on Model A fours.

Is this 1940 or 1955? Timeless hot rods don't tell their age.

Darrel Helms lives in Lakewood, Colorado, and is a member of the Denver Roadsters car club, as is his father, Duane Helms. They had learned about an early roadster hot rod stored in their area. The descriptions they had heard of the car from trusted local hot rodders made them want it badly. They had tried to track it down and buy it for several years, but to no avail. It turned out to be stored in a friend's Quonset hut building only about 10 blocks from Duane's home in Wheatridge, Colorado.

The 1930 Model A roadster was originally built as a racer by Bob Hayes in 1937. Hayes' mother bought the car new in 1930! Hayes' partner Wes Cooper reportedly built the engine for the car and they campaigned it on the dry lakes courses until about 1948.

It was then sold to Bob Learned, who put the car on the street as a hot rod. Learned ran the car on the

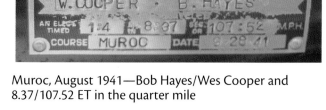

Muroc, August 1941—Bob Hayes/Wes Cooper and 8.37/107.52 ET in the quarter mile

street until about 1956, a logical Helms assumption based on the 1956 California license plate and registration that came with the car. Learned's cousin wound up storing it in his Colorado Quonset.

The Helms duo's several attempts to buy the car were rebuffed. They were told that Learned would never sell the car and that he would also probably never do anything with it, though he had hopes of putting it back on the street. Eventually, in 2002, Duane got a call telling him that the car was finally for sale and that he could make an offer on it. Up to this time, he and Darrel had not actually seen the car, so they made a beeline for the storage building. They pulled the covers off of the car and looked it over. They made their offer, which was accepted, and they were soon the owners of a sure-enough time capsule hot rod.

Having been a race car for 11 years early in its life, and in storage for 46, the roadster doesn't have many miles on it, so it's in pretty good shape and even has what appears to be the original 1930 Ford paint on much of its body. It has obviously been stored inside through most or all of its nearly 75 years, having only spent 15 as a street car.

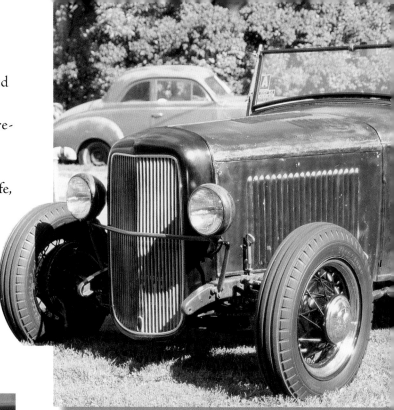

An A-ration sticker from World War II, the Big War.

Obviously there are other projects in the wings at Helms manner. Check the Merc coupe.

As fine a four-banger as you'll find, topped by a Cook Cyclone 4-port head.

Mercury station wagon upholstery covers a homemade seat.

There are plenty of louvers in the folding hood.

'40 Ford brakes and 1940s tow bar attachments.

Since the car has really had just four owners, three of which were bonafide car nuts, its history has been documented and passed on, too. Darrel and Duane not only know what was done to the car to get it to where it is today, they know which owner did it.

The Wes Cooper-built engine is like a display model for early four-cylinder racing engines. The numbers on the block identify it as a 1932 Model B engine. It has a Cook Cyclone 4-port overhead valve head on it, along with a homemade twin-carburetor intake manifold and Stromberg 97 carbs. The dual exhaust header is also homemade. Ignition is via an American Bosch side drive magneto.

After sitting for 46 years, the engine needed to come apart and be rebuilt, which gave its new owners an opportunity to check out the vintage race engine's internal credentials. They were pretty impressive.

The engine sports a Winfield camshaft and a lightened flywheel. It also has a later Ford "C" crankshaft that has been drilled for better oil pressure. It has also been balanced in the bottom end and has a

This view shows the 1941 Mercury steering wheel and instrument panel.

V-8 water pump. Darrel and Duane rebabbited the bearings in the engine, checked all the clearances and bolted the four back together.

The four-cylinder engine isn't a huge powerhouse, though it will thrill. The 1930 rear end is adequate to handle the souped-up power output, though. The transmission is a 1932 case with 1939 gears. The front end is a 1932 Ford commercial axle with a reversed main spring leaf. There are 1940 Ford brakes and as a leftover testament to its dry lakes days, tow-bar mounts on the backing plates.

During the time Bob Learned had the car, he made some modifications toward the hot rod side of life. It was during his time with the roadster that the body was channeled over the frame. He also installed the 1941 Mercury instrument panel into a homemade dashboard. As a safety move, he relocated the fuel tank from the cowl to the rear.

The '30 has a rare accessory rearview mirror with integral clock. The seats are homemade and are covered with Mercury station wagon upholstery. The steering column came from a 1934 Ford. Wheels are 16-inch Kelsey-Hayes wires with

The instrument panel is from a 1941 Mercury.

grooved 5.00 x 16-inch tires on front and block-patterned 8.90 x16-inch rears. The mandatory '32 grille shell completes the look. Other than refreshing the mechanicals and making sure everything was safe, Darrel didn't do much else other than remove bobbed rear fenders that had been added to the car at one time.

Four-cylinder hot rods are unusual these days, so Darrel's A-bone gets a lot of attention. The split header gives it a distinctive roar that tells those in the know that there is definitely something different under the hood.

This car is one of those rare pieces with a history that car guys hear stories about, but no one really knows anyone who has found such a prize. Well, except for those who know Darrel and Duane Helms, that is.

American Bosch side-drive magneto provides spark.

Helms' research hasn't turned up the origin of the SM magneto drive.

CH3

Aaron Mann's Fuelie

1934 Ford Cabriolet

Aaron Mann's 1934 Ford Cabriolet is a true old school hot rod if there ever was one. Except for a few maintenance-related improvements, the car is virtually untouched from when it was built over 40 years ago.

Rear bumper was customized at one time with an added upper center section.

License plate reveals the car's age.

Indianapolis resident Joe Bastian bought the '34 in 1959 and it was already a hot rod by then. When Joe acquired the car, it had a flathead Ford power plant and a straight axle with split wishbones. The body had already been channeled six inches, too.

Joe was a drag racer in the early 1960s, campaigning a 1960 Corvette with a 1956 265 V-8 bored out to 283. It had a '57

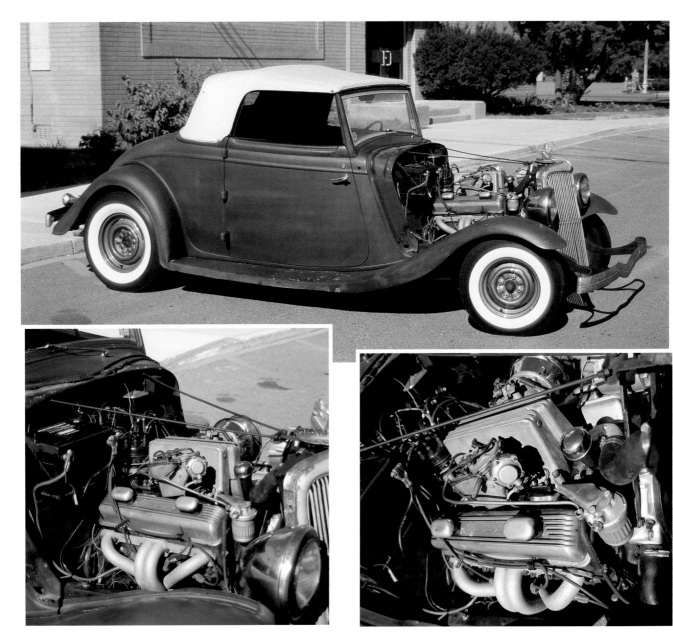

The potent 283 started life as a 265. It was balanced at Precision Balancing in Indianapolis.

The Rochester mechanical fuel injection was massaged by Pete Marriot and runs great.

Corvette fuel injection system and a Borg-Warner T-10 close ratio 4-speed. When the urge to modify the '34 came along, Joe did what any good hot rodder does; he robbed from one car to build another. He took the Chevy drivetrain out of his 'Vette and installed it in the Ford.

The rest of the build parts came from the junkyards surrounding Indianapolis. Joe told Aaron that he would just go to the yards with a tape measure, checking dimensions of various components until he found what he needed. He decided he

needed an independent front suspension since the '34 was his daily transportation. A couple of Corvairs contributed to that need. A 1961 Corvair Spyder donated its suspension and a Corvair Greenbrier van gave up its steering box and column. The Positraction rear end in the car came out of a 1960 Chevrolet and it runs 4.56 gears.

While he was perusing the Corvair department of the local yard, Joe grabbed a set of their bucket seats, too. A 1960 Oldsmobile steering wheel sits on the Greenbrier column and the speedometer is

Corvair bucket seats were a junkyard find 40 years ago.

"Suicide doors" lack any frills or trim.

Aaron's '34 was obviously a green car at one time in its life.

from a Checker cab. The shifter is from an early Corvette. All those jewels were available in junkyards back then. Rather than cut up the instrument panel for the offbeat gauges he used, Bastian simply made mounts to allow them to either float inside or behind the existing holes.

When Joe built the car, he used a heater from an old Plymouth under the right side of the dash (daily driver; Indianapolis winters; any questions?). For the sake of legroom, that has since been removed.

The front fenders and running boards are interesting. They are fiberglass, but homemade. The originals from this very car were used as molds and new ones were laid-up by hand. The rear fenders and gas tank cover are bobbed originals.

The convertible top on the '34 was purchased from Montgomery Ward (remember them?). The car also has a custom rear bumper and a filled cowl vent. When the body was channeled over the frame, the rear quarters and wheelwells were massaged accordingly.

Back to that engine, though. It's a hot little number, sporting 10.5 to 1 pistons and 1961 fuel injection heads, along with a Duntov cam. It has a now-rare W&H DuCoil ignition, an aluminum flywheel and hydraulic clutch.

Precision Balancing Company did the balancing job on the engine way back when. They are still in business and located just east of the Indianapolis Motor Speedway. Precision is one of several old automotive performance companies located

The independent front suspension came from a Corvair donor in the early 1960s.

Dashboard is original '34, and gauges have been adapted to fit without cutting.

in the vicinity of the Speedway, having catered to Brickyard racers, as well as to those racers who run various classes at Indianapolis Speedrome and Raceway Park.

When Joe Bastian's daughter Karen was in high school, Joe gave the car to her and it was her daily driver for a few years. She finally decided to sell it and that's where Aaron Mann came into the picture.

Aaron was in Indianapolis with his dad, attending the Goodguys Indy Hot Rod Happening. They were driving along one of the streets in town and happened across the '34 Cabriolet with a for sale sign on it. They pulled a U-turn and went back to check it out. Aaron fell in love with the car right away and they made the deal on the spot.

Checker cab speedometer is centered behind a 1960 Oldsmobile steering wheel.

The blue oval Ford logo, V-8 symbol and grille are vintage Ford items from 1934.

Sealed beam conversions in original 1934 headlight buckets are an early accessory.

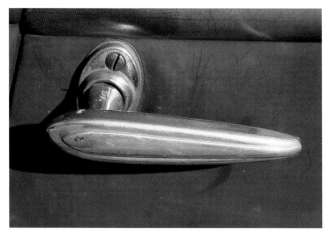

The 1934 Ford door handle is streamlined and simple.

Once Aaron got the car home, he and Dad went through it, replacing some old, worn-out components and generally giving it a dependability and safety refreshing. Aaron says that when he got the car, "…the newest parts on it were the tires from 1966."

Naturally, the '34 got some new tires and brake shoes, along with replacements for all the normal wear expendable items on the engine. He also redid the exhaust system and radiator and added a few of his own personalized touches—a devil hood ornament, a surfer's foot gas pedal, and a very-fitting Indy tag for the license plate.

The idea of dealing with the Corvette's mechanical Rochester fuel injection makes some grown mechanics cringe, but there is a local expert on such monsters right in Aaron's Detroit area backyard. Pete Marriot had the old fuelie dialed in quickly and it runs like the proverbial top.

To his credit, 20-something-year-old Aaron Mann recognizes the significance of the piece of automotive history he now owns. His plans for the car are simple, drive it and preserve it.

It won't be changed and it won't be "restored." It deserves to be left alone and enjoyed.

CH4

Bill Couch's
Dream Car
'34 Ford Coupe

The sculptured lines of a hot rod vision.

Joaquin Arnett (yes, *that* Joaquin Arnett), Andy Granatelli (yes, *that* Andy Granatelli), Bill Couch (yes, *that*, well you get the picture). What do all these men have in common? They are the only three people who have owned this car since 1950. Couch holds the record, though, since he's owned it since 1953!

Like many 1950s teenage boys smitten by the car bug, Detroit area gearhead Bill Couch grew up looking at hot rod magazines, reading them over and over (and over and over), noting which cars he liked best, and the features

that attracted his interest. He would cut out pictures of his favorites and stick them up on the wall in his room.

One of the cars that caught his fancy was a 1934 Ford coupe that he saw in the first issue of *Honk!* magazine. It was built by Joaquin Arnett of San Diego Bean Bandits fame. The car was radical, having been chopped, sectioned, and shortened by Arnett in 1950

and 1951. There was no mention in the article of who owned the car, or Arnett, or even where the picture was taken. There was only one picture of the car, but Couch was in love.

In 1953, Bill Couch was in boarding school. The father of one of his friends owned the Motherwell Lincoln-Mercury dealership in Chicago. One day while they were out driving on the south side of Chicago, Bill spotted a cream colored '34 coupe on a used car lot. They went back to check it out. After looking it over

Possibly one of two Camblers car club plaques left.

The 1934 Ford dream coupe. The Allard sports car suspension

The Allard sports car suspension was adapted by Granatelli in 1952.

from top to bottom, Bill realized it was the same car in the *Honk!* picture he had hanging on his bulletin board at home!

A 16-year-old had no money then, just as today, so Bill called his dad to see if he would loan him the money to buy it. Bill doesn't recall the exact amount required, but believes it may have been around $1,100. That was quite a bit of money in 1953.

Surprisingly, with a little intervention assistance from Mr. Motherwell, his dad agreed.

Bill later learned the car had wound up in Chicago because of the man who bought it from Arnett, none other than Andy Granatelli. When Arnett built the car, it was black. Granatelli saw it at the LA Motorama and bought it from him. Granatelli took it back to his race shop in Chicago and worked the engine over, adding Grancor heads and a few other goodies. He also had the car repainted a cream color.

When Couch got the coupe back to Michigan, he did what all Detroit area boys did then. He drag raced on Woodward Avenue. He also learned to replace and rebuild transmissions through the tried and true teaching tool of repetition. The Granatelli hot-rod flathead ate transmissions like they were candy. Bill kept getting stock Ford gears from his local Ford dealer and the car kept eating them. Once he finally switched to Lincoln Zephyr gears, things held up a little better.

Over the years, the coupe was replaced in Bill's priority list by college, family obligations, and career responsibilities. Thankfully it never left his possession, though, and there was always a place on the family farm to store it inside. It often shared barn space with his Deuce roadster (see Chapter 8).

In 1996, Bill decided it was time to restore the old beauty. He had always loved the car and wanted to enjoy it again. It was his first car, and also the one he taught his wife, Ellen, how to drive in. He asked around to find the top area people to handle the various aspects of the restoration. Mark Kirby at Motor City Flathead in Dundee got the nod for the engine rebuild and Bill says

Dashboard has rare convex lenses and winged S-W gauges.

Seats were restitched in original parchment and avocado vinyl.

Only full-size tires hint at the 1934's reduced size.

it runs flawlessly. It certainly sounds great.

The upholstery was handled by Scott "Willie" Pert and Bill says he did a masterful job of matching the parchment and avocado vinyl that was in the car originally. Willie did the whole job, including the headliner, in one long weekend. No

one knows if there was any sleep on his agenda that weekend.

The bodywork was restored to its former glory by a recommended metal crafter in nearby Mt. Clemens, Paul Reitter. Reitter soon found that Joaquin Arnett had been a master metal worker. The original work was extremely well done with

Attempted section of a '34 grille on the left with stock on the right.

Granatelli-massaged flathead ate many transmissions in the 1950s.

A Stromberg tops the Grancor manifold.

From this angle, the car just looks chopped

almost no warpage or need for filler. Finally, the paint was applied in Port Huron at Watters Works. Then Greg Bock laid on the pinstripes.

Couch's restored gem was a hit in its debut showing at the 1998 Detroit Autorama, winning its class. Since then it has also won awards at St. Ignace and at Meadow Brook. Bill has also wisely traveled to California to meet with the two other significant men in his car's life, Andy Granatelli and Joaquin Arnett. They were able to give him some insight into the car's build history, Arnett from the customizing side and Granatelli from the mechanical side.

Horsepower was the name of the game for the Granatelli brothers, so when they worked over Andy's coupe's mill they did it in style. The engine got a bore and stroke to 276 cubic inches and a set of Grancor (Granatelli Corporation) finned aluminum heads. It also received a Grancor dual intake manifold.

The front suspension might be the most interesting Granatelli contribution, though. Andy (with some likely assistance from brothers Joe and Vince) installed an independent front set-up from a British Allard sports car. The apparatus includes a split swing axle. The Allard brakes and hubs were also adapted to the Ford, allowing the use of the stock wheels.

Couch's '34 coupe looks as good as it ever has, probably better. The car looks, from all angles, like a scaled down '34 Ford. Except for the width, all other proportions have been altered, including the 11 inches that Arnett took out of the length, and four inches that the top was chopped. The hood sides are solid and the top has been filled.

Inside, the cockpit is naturally a little cramped. The glass-knobbed shifter is a shortened '39 Ford piece. The steering wheel came from a 1950 Chevy (new when the car was first built). Very rare convex lens Stewart Warner gauges share dash space with a Jaeger speedometer and clock.

Bill Couch's preserved masterpiece is a significant part of automotive history. Its having been owned early in its hot rod life by Andy Granatelli cements that. The fact that Joaquin Arnett built it, and built it so masterfully, probably helped assure its long life. And Bill Couch, a Michigan hot rod player in his own right, has made some wise decisions regarding this car.

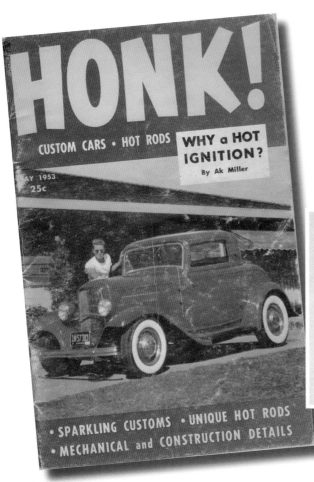

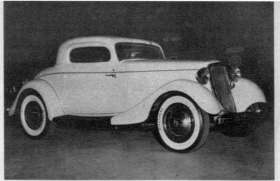

• Classic street coupe was sectioned and chopped to reduce height; is fully equipped for road use.

Couch's love at first sight was profiled inside issue #1 of *Honk!* magazine.

"Regret" – Dennis Lesky's
1932 Ford Sedan

This old gal has been around the block a few times. She's been treated rough, but she's also been in loving hands for many of her long years. One of the cool things about her past is that it has been passed on from owner to owner, so for at least the past 50 years, we can know what has transpired.

Michigan has always been a hotbed of automotive activity. It is, after all, the home of the American and, by most accounts, the world's automotive industry. Car guys are car guys. Guys who design and manufacture new cars by day fool with old ones by night and weekend. It's always been

that way and probably always will be. Michigan has always been home to this Ford, and she has an interesting story.

It's hard to imagine now, but back in the 1950s, there were still 1932 Fords in American junkyards. In 1954, mechanic Bill Waddill of Swartz Creek, Michigan, acquired a Deuce sedan

There are many origins for "Regret," the name of this 1932 Ford sedan.

from just such a yard in nearby Linden, Michigan. Quick perspective check: that would be akin to our buying an '83 Crown Vic body from the same yard today, not that big a deal. At least not then. With 50-year-old hindsight, it's a different matter completely.

When Waddill got the car home, he quickly set about making it distinctively his own. One of the first moves was to have local hot rodder Red Abbey chop the top 3- ¾ inches. Not four inches, not 3 ½. It was a just-right

3-¾. He also painted the car gray with white flames and added the car's first of many hot rod engines, an early Olds Rocket. The car became his daily driver.

Bill Waddill was as interesting a character as his car came to be. One of the "works" that he drove back and forth to was as a member of the Buick Racing Team that raced in the Pan American Mexican Road Races in the 1950s. Bill reportedly took the car to Mexico and used it as a parts runner during various legs of the races. He would run the car from checkpoint to checkpoint, repairing damage to the race cars, then charging on to the next stop. Rumors persist that the Deuce was actually faster on some stretches of the race course than some of the race cars it was supporting!

Waddill was a racer at heart, so Bonneville was always a siren call to him. His first trip there resulted in not being allowed to run the car on the course, though. The Southern California Timing Association (SCTA) rules required that cars with "major body modifications" such as a chopped tops have a roll bar installed. The '32 didn't have one, so Bill was unable to make record runs, though he did hang around and use the car as a chase vehicle and push car for other participants' cars.

In 1958, Waddill started running National Hot Rod Association (NHRA) events and picked up Flint, Michigan, based Kustom Equipment as a sponsor. Kustom's colors were red and white, and so were the Deuce's in very short order. By

The original chicken wire supported fabric roof insert is intact.

1946 Ford juice brakes ride inside finned aluminum brake drums.

The straight-five Stewart Warner gauge cluster made Dennis Lesky seek the car out many years ago.

42

"Pontiac 389" lettering on the hood is both a history lesson and a fortune teller. The car will own one again soon.

that time, the Olds engine had been replaced by a much more powerful Chrysler 392 Hemi. A roll bar was also installed, as well as some well-placed concrete under the rear seat area to help with traction.

At the 1958 NHRA National Drags in Tulsa, the car won the B/G title at a speed of 105.88 and was runner-up in the Little Eliminator competition.

The following year, the car was sold to Bill Pierce, who had Ollie Hines' shop plop a 316 cube Pontiac engine into the car. That's also when the steering box was moved in order to clear the Pontiac's starter.

The next few years of history get a little bit fuzzy, but by 1966 the car was in the possession of John Spatrisano. Pontiac engines were John's thing, and he had a doozy, a built 389 out of a 1963 Pontiac that had been rolled. That engine was the impetus for the car's appearance today.

That Stover and Company-built 389 was a piece of work. It reportedly had a Crower roller camshaft, a balanced crankshaft and pistons, and just about anything else that could have been done in those days. Spatrisano reportedly had over $7,000 tied up in

that drivetrain. That's $7,000 in 1966 dollars (or more than $41,000 today). Dallas Jenks did most of the driving as he and John raced the car all over the Upper Midwest.

That is when the "389 Pontiac" lettering was added to the hood and "Regret" on the doors; "Regret" because they regretted having tied-up that much money in one engine.

Lesky's '32 sedan was a participant in the 1958 Nationals and still wears the participant's decal.

Sparse by today's street rod standards, the interior is all business, family-size drag racer style.

Dennis Lesky is a member of the Headers Car Club.

In 1971 the car passed to Jim Lischkge, who pulled the Pontiac engine and installed a 327 Chevy engine. He owned it until 1979. That's when it came home to the current owner, Dennis Lesky, who has no intention of ever passing it to anyone but his son. Dennis had seen the car a few years before and had tried to buy the dashboard out of it for the Stewart Warner instrument panel and 1958 NHRA Nationals decal.

Dennis had a '32 Victoria at the time, which he had been working on for several years. The lack of progress on the Vicky had him a little discouraged and he was ready for a larger car to accommodate the family that had grown some since the Vicky's beginning days. He paid $3,950 for it.

Over the past 26 plus years, "Regret" has traveled thousands upon thousands of miles. Dennis and his family have taken the car on numerous trips to various hot rod events in the eastern half of the U. S. It always draws a crowd and it's amazing how many people remember it from its early iterations, either when Bill Waddill owned it or when it was raced by Spatrisano and Jenks.

These days this red orange bonafide survivor car resides in Ionia, Michigan, and is the well-known calling card for Dennis Lesky's Ionia Hot Rod Shop. It is temporarily powered by a 350 Chevy engine out of a dump truck, but Dennis promises that it will once again get the 389 Pontiac engine it deserves, and soon. A four-speed will replace the Turbo 350 automatic at the same time. That seems to be what the car should have in it since much of its better known history, and its current paint job, reflect that period.

It looks the part of a vintage drag racer, too, wearing its Halibrand wheels. These days they are shod with modern radial tires, though, as the car gets driven a bunch on Michigan's less than perfect roads.

Dennis Lesky has wisely and thankfully resisted any temptation to restore the car or to change it to any extent beyond drivability and safety. It still has the original seats and the original chicken wire-supported fabric top insert. The top leaks a little…OK, a lot…but it is part of the personality and charm of the car. Putting a new piece in there or, God forbid, a solid insert, would be sacrilegious on a car like this and would ruin it forever.

The vintage paint job wears faint shadows of former sponsors' lettering and dozens of hard-earned paint chips. Count those as badges of honor for a car that has traveled thousands upon thousands of miles over many years on the road. Driving it is like a throwback to another era because it hasn't really been substantially updated in decades.

Slip into the '32 seat and behind the '40 Ford steering wheel mounted on a homemade column and it could be 1955. The rare Champion horn button won't belie that impression. The front brakes and the suspension are vintage Ford hot rod pieces. The brakes are 1946 Ford units in Buick finned drums. Suspension is what Dennis describes as "really flat Ford stuff," a mix and match set-up of whatever was available at the time and would work together.

Windows are drag race style screw-in Lexan, including the back one, which is green. Dennis describes the ventilation system as "bi-level A/C." It consists of a tilt-out windshield and a cowl vent.

Nothing says racin' like a set of Halibrands.

1940 Ford steering wheel is plugged with unusual Champion spark plugs emblem.

"Regret" – Dennis Lesky's 1932 Ford Sedan

45

Lesky's rear bumper is mostly a verbal plea.

Stock '32 Ford taillights are stylish and hard to beat for the proper look.

Though potent and dependable enough, the Chevy engine will soon give way to a 389 Pontiac. It's in the car's roots.

"Regret" is what you might call a moving time capsule. It has been in the care of loving enthusiasts over the course of more than fifty years. Each of those put his mark on the car, yet none beyond Bill Waddill radically altered it. Its current caretaker is the worthy successor to those earlier men.

Dennis Lesky has a discernable reverence for the car and its history and vows to maintain its glory and even return a bit of it.

A tried and true Ford 9-inch rear end has served the Deuce well for many, many years.

Vern Holmes' Short-Timer Deuce
(1932 Ford)

A quick perusal of Vern Holmes' 1932 Ford 3-window coupe will reveal that it is in pretty darned good shape for an old gal of almost 75. The thing is that this car only has 51,000 actual miles on it. And it has spent more time in storage than in use!

Vern says that car went into storage in 1957 and remained there for 42 years. When he bought it in 1999, it appeared basically as you see it here, a well-preserved 1950s hot rod. Forty-two years of idleness can be a little hard on fluids and rubber and such, so Vern went through all systems on the car, replacing normal wear type items. They hadn't worn, but they had certainly aged!

So, the car got all new fluids and fittings, tires and wires. Besides the treads, it got new threads. LeBarron Bonney mohair upholstery and carpet went onto the original seat and floor. The steering column in the car is the original '32, as is the instrument panel. The steering wheel is a 1937 Ford banjo wheel. There is also an accessory rear window blind.

The engine in the car is a stock 1951 Ford 8BA flathead running a stock ignition and intake. The transmission is out of a 1934 Ford and it transmits the power back to a stock '32 rear axle running 4.11 gears. Vern

1940 Ford hydraulic brakes replaced the mechanical 1932 version long ago.

The '51 flathead V-8 is at home in this "Deuce."

Vintage Echlin voltage ballast resides next to a Lowry AFB Drag Strip timing tag.

Vern is a longtime member of the Denver Timing Association.

Apparently the Deuce was a participant in the 1955 NHRA Regional Drags.

has plans to switch the transmission for a 1939 version filled with Lincoln gears in a short time. The transmission is all ready to be installed whenever he gets the free time to do it.

About the only non-stock components on the engine are the Red's headers which feed spent exhaust gases through twin Smithy's mufflers. As was often done on early hot rods, the original hot rodder replaced the stock

The Deuce coupe shines in this natural setting.

The original 1932 dash and gauges are intact on Vern Holms' coupe.

The interior of the '32 includes a banjo steering wheel.

One is for being a contestant at the 1955 NHRA Regional Drag Races and the other is a timing tag from Lowry Air Force Base's drag strip, showing a speed of 82.41 MPH in the timed mile.

The wide whitewalls look right in their 6.70 x 15 and 8.20 x 15 front to rear bias. Even the paint looks right in its original brush-applied blue green hue, accented by a few more recent primer spots where Vern repaired a little surface rust damage. Even the '33 Ford blue dot taillights are correct. The grille shell has been filled and the hood louvered.

mechanical brakes with 1940 Ford hydraulic ones. The suspension is basically stock with the exception of a Mor-Drop front axle.

Get Vern's Deuce away from any other date-identifying surroundings and it looks like it could be 1956 right now. The original 1956 State of Colorado inspection sticker is still on the windshield and it shows 49,241 miles. On the firewall are a couple of competition plaques.

The Moon tank on the front spreader bar harkens back to the Deuce's drag racing days.

This view is pure 1950s hot rod with Moon tank, bucket headlights and whitewalls.

Original 1956 State of Colorado safety inspection sticker on the windshield.

Mileage on the coupe in June of 1956 was only a little over 49,000.

Vern has been around hot rodding and racing most of his years. He is one of the many lifers in the hot rodding community around the Denver/Colorado Springs area. His garage is filled with great memorabilia and even greater cars. That collection includes a former Kenz & Leslie Deuce racer that he has transformed into a slick street rod.

Vern is a member of the Denver Timing Association, the Denver Roadsters, and Early Ford V8 Club. The man knows his early Fords.

Anyone wishing to build a period correct 1950s hot rod could use Vern Holmes' 3-window as a textbook. It *is* a 1950s hot rod.

The Golden Nugget—Jordon/Hines

1934 Ford Cabriolet

The hot rodding world is a tight-knit network of family, friends, and friends that seem like family. In many cases, that is a *very* good thing. In certain instances it's almost divine. It means that special cars like the Golden Nugget 1934 Ford get to survive and be enjoyed by succeeding generations of rod fans.

In late 1952, Detroit area butcher Marty Ribits acquired a somewhat rusty and beat-up 1934 Ford cabriolet. Marty was a hot rodder and custom car enthusiast, so in addition to addressing the Ford's repair needs, he set out to make his '34 into the best of both worlds, a custom hot rod.

One of the top customizers working the Detroit area was a young man named Bill Hines. Ribits took the Ford to Hines' shop and the two laid out their plans for the car's transformation.

Ribits had the will and Hines had the skill to make the car into a radical, yet tasteful and drivable, showpiece.

The car's body was channeled six inches over the frame and then other body components were adjusted accordingly so that the proportions remained aesthetically correct. Those modifications included sectioning the grille by a matching six inches. Custom rocker panels were created to cover the channeling. The rear tail panel under the trunk lid was sectioned by three

In profile, the Golden Nugget's proportions are perfect even though Hines and Jordon modified every panel.

The 1956 Buick Nailhead has a Weiand manifold, three Rochester two-barrels.

Bill Hines turned then-new '55 Chevy headlights upside down.

and a half inches and the rear fenders were moved up the same amount. The car was painted a rich burgundy.

At that time, Marty's '34 was powered by a 286 cubic inch Mercury Flathead with three

deuces. It had a beautiful black and white rolled and pleated interior that Bill Hines recalls was done by a local upholsterer named Curly.

Like many hot rod and custom owners of the day, Marty's life seemed to revolve around that car. He made running changes to it and the timetable for each one is a little bit unclear. Early photos help

a little, but they are undated, so some of the scenario is played out in fading memories and documented by those photographs.

As an example, the earliest available photo, taken at the Ford Rotunda car show, shows a smiling young Ribits standing next to his car. In that photo, the front fenders are short, but the 1955 Chevy headlights have already been installed. Bill Hines recalls those having been done sometime in the winter of 1954 and 1955. Other changes to the car that show up in later photos had not yet taken place, though.

About those headlights— the 1955 Chevrolets caused quite a sensation on many fronts and one of their more popular features came to be the headlights. Their slightly hooded rims found their way onto many custom cars of the day, but Bill Hines took a slightly different approach (as he often did). He turned the headlight housings

upside down and blended them into the Ford's fenders, mid-'30s Pierce-Arrow style, but tunneled.

Apparently not too long after that, the front end was reworked a little more, extending the front fenders down behind the bumper. Hines formed a smooth custom pan that blended with the fenders and extended out to the bumper. The car appeared in the August 1955 issue of *Car Craft* in that form.

In 1956, Marty Ribits purchased a brand new 322

Rear view (top) or rear 3/4-profile (below) show this beautiful car.

Hudson taillights are from a 1949 or 1950 model.

The wheel covers on Golden Nugget are from a 1956 Lincoln Continental Mk II.

The golden hood is graceful and practical with its louvers.

The cloisonné enameled badge is one of Larry Jordon's little touches.

A distinguishing feature is the molded pan between the bumper, fenders and grille.

cubic inch Buick Nailhead V8 and installed it in place of the Mercury Flathead. That mill was adorned with lots of chrome and wore a four carburetor setup.

Marty had a close friend named Ernie Szelesi who was also a hot rodder and custom car fan. He, too, had a '34 Ford similar to Marty's. Szelesi liked the work that Bill Hines had done on Marty's car so well, that

A rare 1954 Ford accessory wheel sits atop a custom made chrome steering column.

Few hot rods, old school or new, have this stylish appearance.

Larry Jordon usually runs the Nugget with a hood; Marty Ribits ran it without.

Black and white tuck and roll interior features 1953 Pontiac exterior moldings on doors.

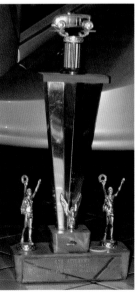

The 1958 Detroit Autorama trophy for best Altered Street Roadster.

he planned to make his car into a clone of Marty's.

Somewhere around that time, a white and black diamond tuck custom interior was installed in Marty Ribits' car. The previous tuck and roll interior was pulled out in its entirety and wound up in Ernie Szelesi's clone-in-waiting.

As a record to that fuzzy time when all of those extended second round changes were made, there is one photograph of the car with the '55 Chevy lights, the extended fenders and front pan, the Buick engine, and the diamond tuck interior, and in its new green paint. It was nicknamed "Sweet Pea." Reportedly, most of Marty's friends and fellow hot rodders

The burgundy version of the car appeared in *Car Craft*, August 1955.
Photo courtesy Larry Jordon and Car Craft

Marty Ribits was fairly tall, a clue to the Golden Nugget's not being chopped.
Photo courtesy Larry Jordon

did not like the new green paint and as hot rodders tend to do, they told him so. Sweet Pea was a short-lived iteration of the car.

Sweet Pea made another trip back to Bill Hines' Custom Shop and emerged as the Golden Nugget. According to Hines, local paint supplier Richard Mason ordered the new metallic gold and clear lacquer out of Chicago. The new gold paint proved to be a better choice and suited the car very well, adding an air of classiness that garnered it many awards and several magazine appearances, including the July 1958 *Custom Cars* and the March 1960 *Cars*. The Golden Nugget also won the first place trophy for Altered Street Roadster at the 1958 Detroit Autorama.

Continuing work was done on Szelesi's 1934 Ford, too, but Bill Hines moved his custom shop to California before it could be completed. It did receive a gold paint job to match that of the Golden Nugget and came to be named Goldbrick. The car has been owned for some time by Bob Larivee, Sr. of International Show Car Association and Detroit Autorama fame. That original Golden Nugget tuck and roll interior is still in the Goldbrick, and still looks pretty good for its 50 years.

Over the ensuing years, Marty Ribits drove the Golden Nugget, showed it at various shows, and garnered many awards. As often happens, other interests and other cars eventually supplanted the '34

and it wound up sitting in a field and slowly deteriorated.

One of the early admirers of the Golden Nugget was Jackson, Michigan, resident Larry Jordon. Jordon's love for customs and hot rods was influenced to a great extent by those 1950s Detroit Autoramas and the cars that made up the shows. A car guy to the core, he became a body man and customizer himself. In fact, he was doing custom work while he was in high school. Occasionally the opportunity would arise to do a paying custom job such as frenching some headlights or installing some custom taillights on a school day. On those days he would skip class and make a few bucks doing what he loved to do instead.

As the Golden Nugget, the car appeared in the March 1960 *Cars* magazine.

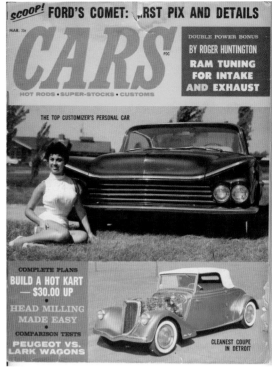

Larry and Marty Ribits became friends and Larry often tried to buy Marty's slowly deteriorating custom masterpiece, but no sale. Jordon was persistent enough that there was no doubt that Marty knew he wanted the car, though. A few years ago Marty became terminally ill. Having no children of his own (he had been single all but a few months of his life), Marty willed the Golden Nugget to his nephew, Ray Lovasz. Ray is a gearhead in his own right and had always wanted to see the Golden Nugget restored to its former glory. Marty's one stipulation in willing the '34 to Ray was that if Ray decided not to restore the car, he would pass the car on to Larry Jordon. After owning it for three years, Ray acknowledged that he would never get around to doing anything with the Golden Nugget, so he passed it on to Larry.

Larry's plan all along, should he ever to come to possess the Golden Nugget was to restore it to its show winning glory. He and his wife Sandy set a goal to have the Golden Nugget ready to debut at the 2005 Detroit Autorama in early March. The Autorama unveiling was significant because the car's original builder, Bill Hines, was scheduled to be the featured builder at the Autorama. That debut date meant that Larry would have to work all winter to get it done. They didn't realize what an undertaking that was going to be.

Years of sitting in a field had definitely taken their toll on the former beauty. Larry soon found that a complete bare metal restoration was in store, as was replacement of many of the body panels.

Larry builds custom cars and hot rods for other people at his shop, Larry Jordon Enterprises, by day, so work on his own car had to be performed by night and on the weekend. He soon found that 16- and 18-hour days were the norm.

Jordon took scrupulous measurements of every part of the car before starting disassembly. He measured all the various panels and their adjacent pieces, studied how everything worked together, and wrote it all down.

As he disassembled the car, Larry learned a little bit about

The Golden Nugget early in Larry Jordon's restoration process.
Photo courtesy Larry Jordon

1950s custom work. He said he had unbolted a front fender and started to lift it off but it wouldn't move. He thought he had left a bolt in it, so he looked all the bolt holes over and all were empty. He gave the fender another, stronger tug and it finally moved. Sometime over the car's life, several dents had been filled with lead. The fender weighed 80 pounds!

Rebuilding the Golden Nugget consumed all of Larry Jordon's free time during the winter of 2004 and 2005. He even spent most of the day on Thanksgiving out in the shop. A couple of times he became discouraged at all the work that lay before him and was ready to throw in the towel, but Sandy encouraged him and they both agreed that the Nugget was a significant car that needed to be completed and preserved.

One cannot appreciate the amount of work and the extensive modifications that Bill Hines put into the Golden Nugget and that Larry Jordon had to replicate. Jordon's reverence for the car and its original builder, and the desire to retain its heritage, came into play several times as he was building it. Opportunities for shortcuts were not taken.

Because of all the extensive work originally done by Hines and his keen eye for proportion, many of the parts on the car that look stock are not quite so. A case in point is the hood. It needed to be lengthened by a scant one and a half inches to make everything fit together correctly between the cowl and grille shell.

The Golden Nugget (left) sits beside the as yet un-gold Goldbrick on a dreary Michigan day.
Photo courtesy Larry Jordon

Well, the Golden Nugget was indeed finished in time for the 2005 Autorama and it was a huge hit. Larry Jordon was bestowed the highly coveted Meguiar's Preservation Award for his efforts.

The real award was less tangible, though. That was the approval of Bill Hines, the Golden Nugget's creator. When Larry walked over to Hines' display area, introduced himself, and told Bill that he had restored the car and that is was there at the show, the first thing Bill said was, "Which interior did you put in it?" When he found out that Larry had put the tuck and roll in rather than the diamond patterned one, he was pleased. Bill said he had never liked the diamond one.

The Golden Nugget with the universally less-favored diamond tuck interior.
Photo courtesy Larry Jordon

Bill spent quite a bit of time at the Autorama looking the car over from every angle. He told Larry that the Nugget was always one of his favorite cars and his love for the car was apparent. His eyes still gleam when he talks about the car. He told Larry that the car looked better than it ever had. That's quite a compliment coming from the guy who created the gorgeous car originally.

Bill Hines at the 2005 Detroit Autorama with the beauty he'd created over 50 years before.
Photo courtesy Bill Hines

CH8

"'32 Skidoo" - Bill Couch's

'32 Ford Roadster

Couch's roadster looks much like it did in 1957. Taillights are '48 Chevy blue dots.

Thirty-two Fords are the quintessential hot rod. That is certainly not a recent development in the world of hot rodding either. They've been so since about, oh, 1933. This car didn't come along in hot rod form quite that early, but it did happen a long time ago; 1955 to be exact. And it was built into a hot rod by the same guy that owns it now, Bill Couch.

In 1955, Michigan native Bill Couch was a freshman college student at the University of Arizona. He bought the '32 roadster during that first year of school. Bill already had a hot rod heart at that young age. In fact, he already had a hot rod back home,

and a pretty significant one at that. (See Chapter 4.)

Back in the 1950s, college freshmen at most schools were not allowed to keep cars on campus and the University of Arizona was no exception to that practice. Consequently, Bill kept the roadster in a garage a mile away from campus and paid 10 bucks a month for the privilege. Having no other car for transportation, Bill either bummed a ride from buddies or walked between the garage and campus. That rented garage was home to the car for two years and it was there that Bill Couch transformed an innocent '32 Ford roadster into the hot rod he has owned for over 50 years.

When the transformation was complete, he had a hot little roadster. It sported a 1948 Ford flathead backed up with a '39 gearbox. It had the requisite big and little tires on steel Ford rims. Charlie Hall filled and peaked the grille shell and also filled the air vent on the cowl. Well-known sprint car fabricator, driver, and Hall of Famer Granvel "Hank" Henry created the dropped tube axle and matching wishbones.

A hot rod cockpit, mid-1950s style, is a sparse office indeed.

In the summer of 1957, Bill shipped the roadster back home to Michigan, along with several other personal belongings including some spare parts he had acquired for the '32. It was during that shipment that the movers "lost" the hood for the car. The pink hood that resides on the car now was a spare that Bill had picked up at a swap meet in Arizona or nearby. It still wears the handwritten identification markings originally scrawled by the movers in 1957 in addition to their inventory tag.

While Bill went back to school, his brother decided to take Bill's '32 drag racing. He gutted the body to make it as light as possible and even took out many of the body's braces. Local hot rod legend Bill Waddill built a bored and stroked '56 Chevy engine and that was put into what had become a 1932 Ford roadster race car, replacing the Ford Flathead.

Says Couch, "We only had one drag strip at that time, New Baltimore Dragway. The car was fast but he generally got beat in the last race by Connie Kalitta. That happened many times." Kalitta's constant thrashing of the roadster led to a change of race cars.

Bill goes on. "My brother pulled the engine and built a new race car from a Crosley. The roadster was stripped of race parts

The surplus aluminum fighter seat was purchased for $3 some 50 years ago.

Seat tag has supplier information, date of manufacture, intended use (P-51D fighter).

Take notes. This is what a hot rod Deuce looked like 50 years ago.

and spent the next 40 years being moved from one barn to another on our farm."

The motivation for resurrecting the '32 came in the form of the Detroit Autorama. When Bill's longtime friend and Autorama boss Bob Larivee told him that one of the features of the 2005 Autorama would be a traditional old school hot rod section, they both knew what had to be done and who were the right guys to do it.

Bill Couch doesn't do much wrenching these days, although he certainly hasn't lost the touch. His life is a little more relaxed now that he's retired from the automotive fastener business, so if the '32 was going to be completed in time to make its second debut at the 2005 Autorama, someone with a little more respect for deadlines was going to have to spin the tools. Not a problem at Couch Manor.

The mill is a stock 1949 Ford version of Henry's Flathead.

Bill has passed on the gearhead gene in huge proportions to his two sons, Billy and John. Billy is a highly-acclaimed professional motorsports artist with a love and appreciation for fine machinery in the Formula One and exotic sports car fields. He is a skilled mechanic as well. Brother John actually restores classic cars for a living. We're talking concours-level restorations. Having grown up with Dad's roadster a regular and permanent family fixture, these gents were definitely on board to resurrect the ol' family heirloom.

What's as important and refreshing as the willingness and skill level John and Billy possess is the understanding they share regarding the historical significance of the car that has been entrusted to them. Both agreed that the '32 should be returned to its mid-1950s state with as little alteration as possible. As preserved in the various Couch family barns and garages over the past 50 years, the roadster was one of those rare cars that is simply too good to restore. Though John restores 100-point cars for wealthy collectors every day, Dad's roadster needed special treatment.

So, John rebuilt and adjusted the original mechanical brakes so that they work like they were intended to. A certain author was "treated" to a hair-raising trip through an as yet unpopulated subdivision near the Couch homestead during the research for this book and can attest to the fact that the brakes do, indeed, work extremely well. In fact, they

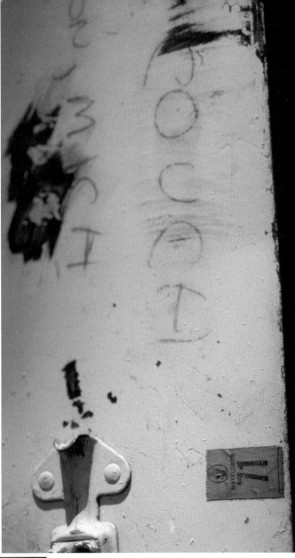

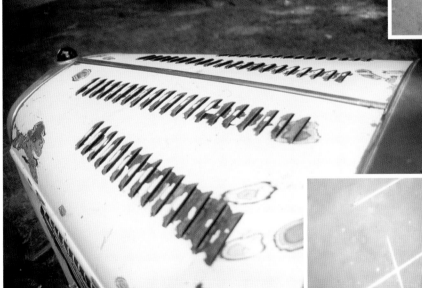

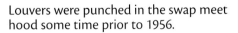

Louvers were punched in the swap meet hood some time prior to 1956.

Mayflower Moving inventory tag is still on the hood, as is the owner's name and city.

Original louver layout lines are intact on the underside of the hood.

The front view shows the car's nose (top) and the a view of the engine (top right) with the hood open.

work much better than the passenger side door latch on the reduced-bracing body.

Because the faded pink hood has such an interesting story, it was left untouched, too. Besides the mover's markings on the outside, it also has the layout lines for the louvers on the inside surface of the upper sections.

The interior is about as basic as it gets. In other words, it's hot rod style. The driver's seat is a surplus aluminum one for a P-51D WW2 fighter airplane that Bill picked up at Davis-Monthan Air Force Base in Tucson around 1956. He paid $3 for it. The passenger seat is out of a '32 Ford sedan.

This fenderless Ford roadster shows its rugged front end.

The car looks pretty much the way it did in 1957 when it arrived in Michigan. It has a 1949 Ford Flathead in it instead of the '48 mill that Bill originally used, but otherwise, it's as if it had never

Guide headlights (top), with parking lights (below), have long been a hot rod favorite.

The Pine's Winter Grille can be shut off to restrict air flow through the radiator in winter.

been taken apart by Bill's drag racing brother all those years ago. It still has the '48 Chevy blue dot taillights and all the stock Ford running gear. One extremely rare piece on the car is the working Pine's winter grille. Its louvers can be closed, allowing the car to run warmer in cold Michigan winters.

Yes, the car was ready in time to make the Autorama and it was a huge hit with the crowds there. All three Couches spent many hours telling the story of the car to interested listeners. And TV hostess Courtney Hanson chose it as her pick among the traditional hot rods. Maybe it was the pink hood.

CH9

Joe Haska's

Sweetheart '34 Ford Coupe

The '34 5-window has a classic hot rod stance.

Lucky man Joe Haska was driving this sweetheart of a 1934 Ford 5-window coupe when he went on his first date with his sweetheart. He has owned the car for 44 years and he still has the same sweetheart, too. She's his wife now.

Joe says he bought the car in July of 1963 and paid a whopping $750 for it. Since that time, the car has usually been his daily driver. It has gone through three engines, four paint jobs, plus two interiors and approximately 28 sets of tires. That's a pretty reasonable investment for the privilege of driving one of the coolest cars in Denver, Colorado!

A retired Denver fireman, Joe Haska is a car show promoter. He is the owner of Greybeard Promotions, Inc. His premier event is the Rocky Mountain Rod & Custom Show, held each November in Denver. It seems only fitting that the guy promoting the area's top car show would have such a great car.

The fuel tank cover on Joe Haska's coupe is punched full of louvers.

This low profile shows off the "Sweetheart" Ford.

Small chrome nerf bar offers a little protection for the classic grille.

Classic and tasteful '39 Ford taillights.

Joe's car is a study in the conservative, traditional rod look. He painted it black in PPG Delstar acrylic enamel. It has tasteful red and white stripes along the reveal line. Inside, the Glide seat was covered with black and white leather by Sew Fine Interiors. The white material is in tuck and roll design while the black is smooth. The theme carries to the headliner and door panels as well as the seat. The dashboard is a custom 1933 Ford version. A sprint car style 4-spoke steering wheel sits atop a Lime Works steering column. The Art Deco-style ribbed turn signal switch is also a Lime Works item.

Under the hood is where a hot rod is defined and Joe Haska's '34 is no exception to that rule. The flathead V8 currently in the car, rebuilt by Tom Barton, started life in a 1948 Mercury. It's a 286 cubic inch version with a 3 3/8-inch bore and a 4-inch stroke. The engine has been balanced and utilizes Edelbrock aluminum heads and a ¾ track grind camshaft. The intake manifold is also from the House of Edelbrock and it has a 1956 Thunderbird carburetor with a bell-type air cleaner on top. The ignition came from a 1942 Ford.

The rear end is an 8-inch Ford and the transmission is a five-speed from a Chevy S-10 pickup. All this go-motion apparatus is bolted to a 1934 Ford chassis built by Sonnenfeld Enterprises in Aurora, Colorado. The front brakes came from a 1956 Ford. Wheels are 15-inch steelies with 5.60 front tires and 8.20 rears.

Joe Haska has had several other hot rods and numerous modern cars over the years. They have all come and gone except the trusty old '34. It's still his favorite and the one he drives more than any other car, old or new. It's definitely a sweetheart with staying power.

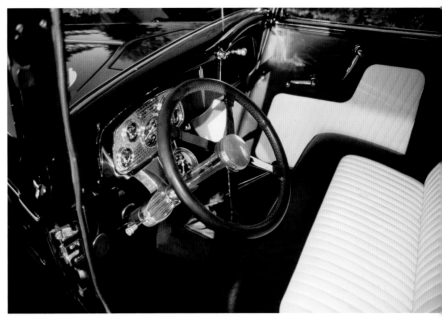

Lime Works steering column and turn signal switch, sprint car wheel.

Joe is a member of the Strippers Car Club in Denver.

The warmed flathead uses Edelbrock heads and intake, T-Bird carb.

Sew Fine interior is tasteful and inviting.

"Generation Spanner"
- Bob Merkt's
'32 Ford Roadster

Bob Merkt, Jr.'s 1932 Ford roadster has been in the family since 1956. Since then its ownership has passed through several different family members, but it has never been outside the Merkt clan.

Bob "Bleed" Merkt is the rightful heir to this cool little automotive silver mine.

assembled the car, channeling the body over a Z'ed frame. The first engine installed in the car was a Flathead V-8. Miles made nerf bars for the rear and had them chrome plated.

Purchased by Bob's grandfather, Francis Merkt, the original package consisted of a '32 frame, some unknown cowl and the back half of a '29 Ford coupe. That's all. Bob's uncle Miles Merkt scrounged up a 1932 Ford Fordor sedan cowl and doors, which he adapted to the existing parts. With Dad's help, Miles

In the late 1950s and early 1960s, the roadster was well-known around the Milwaukee area. Teen heartthrobs, the

Bob made the nerf/spreader bar (top and right) the way "grandpa would have done it."

The Merkt roadster has a classic look as a result of the vintage components and stance.

Headers were made in the 1960s by local exhaust whiz Russ Sacs.

Crescendos, visited to do a local TV show and they actually performed a song in the car.

As often happens with cars of this ilk, Miles lost interest in it and it passed to his brother, Bob Senior. In 1962 he pulled out the tired Flathead and installed an Oldsmobile engine with six carburetors. He ran it in that configuration for about six years. By 1968, most people were putting Chevy engines in their hot rods, so Bob Sr. followed suit and dropped in a 283 with a three-speed.

The 283 didn't suit him (not enough power), so he plopped a big block 396 between the frame rails. That turned out to be too

Bob and his bride took the roadster to Back to the '50s on their honeymoon.

much of a good thing. The extra weight of the big block threw everything out of whack and the car lost its feel of balance. Out came the 396 and in went a 365 horse 327 out of a Corvette. As the lovely Miss Goldilocks would say, "This one is just right."

Senior says he remembers his dad and Miles talking about a car needing to have the right "balance." It needed to look right and it needed to feel right. Through all the Merkt hands that have been on the roadster, balance has always been a goal, and a pretty well-achieved one at that.

Throughout the 1970s, the Merkt-mobile garnered trophy after trophy at various car shows, including the World of Wheels in Milwaukee. Then Bob, Sr. lost interest in the car after awhile, too, and it sat for several years.

OK, Junior's turn! Ownership of the car rightfully passed to Bob Merkt, Jr., about 1990 and he promptly ignored it for 10 years. As Bob points out, "I've never *not* had that car in my life." Familiarity didn't breed contempt, but it didn't breed excitement for the car either, at least not at first. He was involved in his band, "Bleed" from which he has earned the name many know him by, Bob Bleed. He simply didn't make the time to get to the roadster.

Finally, the build-a-car bug bit and Bob went to work on the Deuce, adding his own personal touches. Repair came first, though. The car sat in a leaky garage for 10 years and the uninvited elements had taken their toll.

Several places in the floors were rusted through and there were places throughout the body that had not aged well. So Bob took everything down to bare metal, replaced the floor and laid his healing hands on places in the body that had merely been patched previously. He lowered the car a couple of inches more and fashioned a new front spreader/nerf bar, "…the way my grandpa would have done it." He also chopped the windshield.

The interior looks for all the world like a late 1950s or early 1960s version would have. A 1949 Mercury dashboard was sectioned to fit the narrower '32. If not for the dates some of them wrote with their autographs, even the signatures on the glove box could have been from 40 years ago.

Those names are from the elite of customs and rods – Bill Hines, George Barris, the Alexander Brothers,

and even Ed "Big Daddy" Roth. A metal flake steering wheel sits atop a 1940 Ford steering column. Chris Theames in Madison, Wisconsin, stitched the tuck and roll vinyl interior in a 1950s period-correct design.

Just before the car had last been decommissioned, the 327 engine was yanked and sold to a Corvette restorer. In its place was a tired old 307 stocker. Bob unceremoniously pitched that lump and dropped in a built 301 small block, much more in keeping with the spirit of a hot rod roadster. He wisely kept the custom-built headers that local exhaust guy Russ Sacs built forty years ago. Also in the hot rod tradition, the car has a four-speed manual transmission.

The rear end is from a 1950 Olds, as many were back in the day. Likewise, the early Ford hydraulic

Glove box autographs include Ed "Big Daddy" Roth, George Barris, Bill Hines, A-Brothers

The dashboard is a narrowed 1949 Mercury unit.

Ahh, what a view from the cockpit looking out over the multi-carbed Chevy mill.

Sometimes the roadster wears slicks on steelies, sometimes mags and road tires.

Cadillac taillights from 1959 sit inside a custom rear grille.

brakes that work inside finned Buick drums. They look good and they work very well, especially on a light, minimal car like this one. Bob added some '59 Caddy taillights to the rear. Check out those gauges in the firewall. Those were found at a swap meet and were inspired by a Monogram '32 Ford model from the 1960s. At its appearance in the 2005 Detroit Autorama, Merkt's roadster was constantly surrounded by admiring car nuts. Obviously Bob has continued in the family tradition of maintaining a balanced look for the car. Several spectators were overheard wondering if the car had been built recently or if it was an older build. It's difficult to tell by looking at it as its several traditional features do not give its build-age away.

Call the Merkt Deuce what you will—family heirloom, obsession, or the Bleed roadster. It is a great piece of history and one sweet ride. The car is certainly in very capable and deserving hands. It has appeared in a few magazines over the years and is also featured in the DVD, *Mad Fabricators Society Volume One*. It also gets driven…a lot. In fact, Bob and his new bride took it on their honeymoon last summer. How fitting.

Firewall-mounted redundant gauges were inspired by a model car.

Four Strombergs sit atop a vintage Weiand manifold.

This 1932 Ford roadster is wild and fun.

Bob's Uncle Miles (left) and his buddy Jim Sessady planning their strategy with the original foundation for the rod in the fall of 1956.
Photo courtesy Bob Merkt

By September of 1957, the Merkt rod was a complete, running car. Note the homemade nerf bar and the cycle fenders.
Photo courtesy Bob Merkt

Bob Merkt senior wanted more power than a Flathead could offer. He installed the Olds Rocket in 1962.
Photo courtesy Bob Merkt

August, 1967, and the first iteration of the big chrome headers.
Photo courtesy Bob Merkt

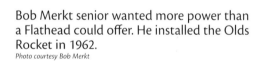

Red Ram Hemi came from a 1955 Dodge.

CH11

"Esmeralda" – She Lives!
Daryl Roberts'

1929 Ford Roadster

There are some old hot rods around that are just so cool, people won't let them die. Esmeralda is just such a car. A staple around the Colorado Springs area for several years, Esmeralda was decommissioned for a long time, but rose from the dust to ride again. Current owner Daryl Roberts had his eye on the car for several years, making sure that he kept track of her whereabouts. When the opportunity arose, he snatched her up.

"Midnight" and "Chief" Castaneda were well known figures in the hot rod and racing world around Colorado Springs, Colorado, in the 1950s and 1960s. Back then there were four gas stations at the intersection of Cache La Poudre and Nevada Street in the Springs. All four were hangouts for the

That Esmeralda – she's a hot little number!

Vintage Southern California Timing Association badge.

Who was she? No one seems to know for sure.

Esmeralda's back on the road and she gets around.

local hot rodders. The Castaneda brothers' hangout of choice among the quartet was a Conoco station, which was owned by a couple of gents named Zecha and Adams. Chief also reportedly worked for Zecha and Adams, at least part time.

It was only natural then that when Midnight and Chief (actually, Theo) decided to build a race car in the early 1950s, sponsorship would come from their buddies at the Conoco station.

According to Roberts' research, for at least part of the car's racing career it was reportedly run as a full-fendered 4-cylinder version at a clay banks track near Colorado Springs. It was said to have been rolled over during that period, resulting in the removal of the fenders (or what was left of them). At about the same time, the engine was replaced with a Ford flathead V8. It has also carried a small block Chevy engine at least two or three times over the years.

As was often the case in the period, Esmeralda is believed to have run in different types of events at different venues. Quite a bit of drag racing and speed trials took place in the Denver area during that time, and slightly foggy memories of some aging area hot rodders recall Esmeralda's presence at some of those events. Most of the details about the car have come from Chief/Theo's son, Paul Castaneda, who still lives in Colorado Springs. A few others have also contributed details. The brothers were reportedly a little wild in their younger days, too, which adds to their notoriety and to the significance of their car, at least in the hearts and minds of local gearheads.

Esmeralda was a feature around the hot rod and racing circles from the early '50s through most of the 1960s. When Chief died in 1968, the car was disassembled and some of the parts scattered to the four corners of the local hot rodding world. Midnight died in 1970.

Esmeralda's carcass passed among a few homes in the ensuing years. Finally in 2004, the car was for sale. That's when Daryl Roberts found out and made his move. He acquired the bones of Esmeralda and began his resurrection process.

Daryl says, "All that was left (of Esmeralda's parts) were two junk '32 frame rails, which I didn't use, and most of the body. The rest was gone."

The left door and right cowl panel somehow remained in the Castaneda family and eventually wound up in Paul's garage. Paul donated those to the cause and was a staunch supporter of Daryl's efforts to return Esmeralda to her former glory. Oddly enough, considering the car's notoriety, no one seems to know for sure where the name came from. Daryl says he's heard that there was a comic book character by that name that was the inspiration, but the real origin is unclear.

When Daryl Roberts acquired Esmeralda, he set about making her a streetable hot rod, maintaining as much as possible of the original flavor of the car, careful not to over-restore or dilute character. He commissioned a chassis from SoCal Speed Shop in California, since what was left of the original was pretty useless anyway. That formed the foundation for what has become a pretty cool updated vintage hot rod.

A MoPar guy to the core, he used a 1955 Dodge 270 cubic inch Red Ram Hemi that he had lying around in the garage. The transmission is a 727 Torqueflite. The rear end is an 8 ¾" Chrysler with 3.31 gears.

The ignition for the Hemi is a Chrysler dual point system, while the pipes and headers were custom made. The Red Ram got an Offenhauser 2 x 2 manifold with a pair of Stromberg 97 carbs.

An open wheel car needs to have a vintage style suspension, so Esmeralda has buggy springs front

Port-a-Walls were the poor man's whitewalls of the 1950s and 1960s.

Dual Stromberg carbs sit atop the Dodge engine.

and rear. The dropped front axle uses disc brakes. The rear brakes are drum. The 15" wheels (front from a Plymouth, rear from a Dodge pickup) are shod with tires wearing vintage Port-a-Walls.

The interior has more Dodge truck stuff in the form of the cut down seat, upholstered by Shelton's Upholstery. When Daryl got Esmeralda, she was still set up as a center-steer car from the racing days. He moved the steering back to the left side, using

a steering column crafted from exhaust tubing. Old racing safety belts finish off the interior. The windshield has been chopped two inches from stock.

It was important to maintain as much as possible from the car's original appearance. Otherwise, Esmeralda wouldn't be Esmeralda, now would she? So Daryl has done just that. Most of the original graphics are in place, touched up in a few places by Chuckie. Rock chips remain as badges of honor and a testament to the fact that this is a driven car. It was for a long time and has been returned to that station in life.

Seeing this car in a crowd brings an appreciation for how much car guys love simple old traditional hot rods. Even Colorado guys who have seen the car several times before walk past more expensive, flashier cars to look Esmeralda over again. People want to sit in it. They walk around it several times just taking in all the details. Yes, that Esmeralda is a crowd pleaser. She's a little hottie

Wind 'er up and let's go!

Buggy sprung Chrysler 8 ¾-inch rear.

The dash includes a vintage timing association tag (right).

'32 Ford grille shell leads the way.

Dennis Brackeen's

Tasteful T

T-buckets were all the rage in the late 1960s and early 1970s. It seemed they were everywhere or at least everywhere the rod magazine photographers went. The majority of the cars looked alike, though.

The turtledeck rear tapers down to the 1948 Chevy taillights.

To be honest, most of them looked like caricatures and cartoon cars. Many had cycle wire front wheels with skinny little tires. In the back, they had huge wide meats that would hydroplane at the hint of rain, maybe even on high humidity days without rain. Usually they had no front brakes.

They had tall two-piece folding windshields and even taller peaked soft tops. It wouldn't have been surprising to see a couple of dozen clowns climb out of one when it pulled up to a curb.

It's no wonder the cars were called fad-T nor that the fad finally fastly faded. Let's all be thankful for that.

Be that as it may, there were a few—very few—Model T based rods built during that period that were actually tastefully proportioned and that did not look like a runaway from Barnum and Bailey's Greatest Show on Earth. One of those cars was built by Wayne Taylor. The car now belongs to Dennis Brackeen of Lakewood, Colorado.

When Taylor built the car, he kept an eye toward proportion and traditional hot rod good looks rather than the ridiculousness of the then-current fad of outlandish one-upsmanship. As a result, he

The 350 Chevy breathes through homemade headers.

The mostly stock engine is plenty powerful for the lightweight T.

built a car that even after 35 years still looks good. That's unusual in the world of T-buckets.

Dennis Brackeen, half of the team of Brackeen and Longwell Racing, has some pretty good taste in cars himself so when this T became available, he scooped it up.

There are a few key ingredients to the look that sets this T apart. For one, the body is channeled over the frame, giving it a low stance. Just as important are the windshield and the top. The windshield is lower than most, a chopped one-piece unit. That restraint carries over in the top that is also lower and lacks the Woody Woodpecker with Butch Wax pointy-back look of many.

The tastefulness continues in the dark blue enamel paint, light blue pinstriping, and white tuck and roll

Dennis Brackeen's T hot rod has a great look from any angle.

Homemade dash carries excellent instrumentation.

White tuck and roll is a nice contrast to the rich blue paint.

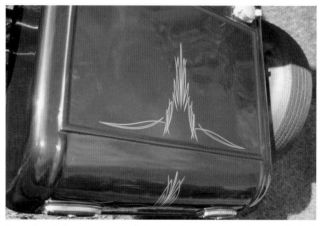

Just the right amount of pinstriping accents the turtledeck.

interior. Tasteful, timeless. The white three-spoke steering wheel is bolted to a Volkswagen bus steering column. A custom-made wood dashboard holds six gauges in easy sight of the lucky driver.

Power for Dennis' rod comes from a Chevy 350 backed by a 350 Turbo HydraMatic. It uses a Mallory ignition system. The exhaust system was garage built. The rear axle is a Chevy 10-bolt.

Good sense prevailed in the choice of wheels and tires for the T. The tires are 5.60 x 15 and 6.50 x 15 front and rear, respectively, mounted on chrome steel smoothie wheels. Brakes on all four corners are from a '53 Chevy.

See, it is possible to build a popular hot rod that will stand the test of time. It just takes some good taste and a little restraint.

CH13

"Love at First Sight" – Dave Kurz's

'28 Sedan Delivery

Englewood, Colorado, automotive artist Dave Kurz fell in love when he was 13 years old. Unlike most boys with their first crush, Dave held out for the one he loved for 40 years. Aw, don't get all misty-eyed. That love was for a car, not some pony-tailed teeny-bopper!

That car – this '28 Ford Sedan Delivery – first appeared to Dave in the July 1965 issue of *Hot Rod Magazine*. Right there, on page 54, was the car that lit Dave's fire. Tex Smith wrote that first article and he waxed eloquently about the fact that the owner, Sepulveda, California's Michael Ray, had less than $1,000 invested in the rod, including the original $200 he paid for the stock delivery.

A thousand bucks? Some wheels cost that much these days…for one wheel! Of course that was $1,000 in 1965 dollars, but still that was a pretty small sum for a classy, finished, *Hot Rod*-worthy car. *Hot Rod* was the tip of the top back then. There was no better magazine for a hot rod to be featured in, period.

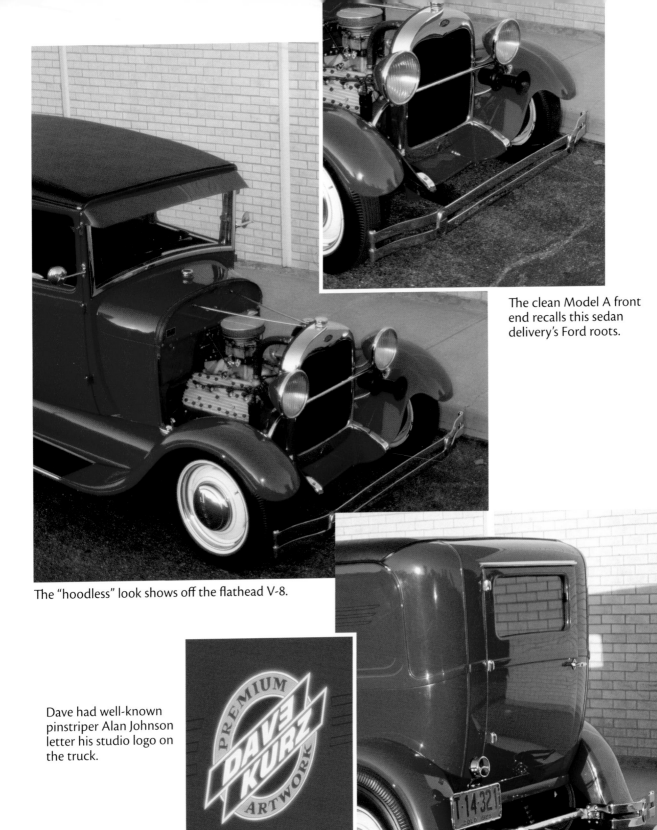

The clean Model A front end recalls this sedan delivery's Ford roots.

The "hoodless" look shows off the flathead V-8.

Dave had well-known pinstriper Alan Johnson letter his studio logo on the truck.

A hot rod with utility – it's hard to beat a sedan delivery.

Note the louver style is rounded on top.

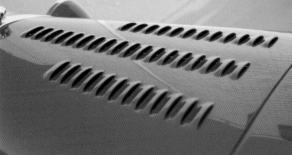

Visors pre-dated tinted windows.

The closed hood brings out the bright red paint scheme.

The late Ford flathead has Edmunds heads and an Edelbrock manifold.

Ray's delivery must have caught lots of people's eyes over the years. It appeared in a magazine again in 1981 and that time it was on the cover of the July issue of *Street Rodder*. Yes, Dave saw that one, too. He was still lusting for the car like he had 16 years before. Some guys never get over that first love.

Dave kept those magazines and would look at the car once in awhile but never really expected it would cross his path. But it did, 40 years after the first time he saw its picture. He heard about the car being for sale and went to look at it. He could hardly believe how little it had changed in all those

The late Ford flathead has Edmunds heads and an Edelbrock manifold.

Roomy interior was upholstered forty years ago, still looks great.

years. It even still had the 40 year-old Roman Red lacquer that Gus Gordon had sprayed for Michael Ray.

Well, of course Dave Kurz bought the car and brought it home. He won't admit it, but there are strong suspicions that he may have stayed in the garage with it at least a couple of nights.

Dave states that the delivery is about 90 percent the same as it was when he first laid eyes on it in 1965. Obviously it has been extremely well cared for. There is a different engine in it now, although it's still a flathead V-8. The current one is a post-1949 with Edmunds heads. It runs through a 1949 Ford truck three-speed transmission to a Ford 8-inch rear end. The engine uses the original Ford ignition system. The headers look to be the same ones as were on the car in 1965, now painted black instead of white. Whereas the car had a tri-power

The '39 Nash steering is mounted Model-T style.

PRACTICAL PANEL

Free delivery? No, but this inexpensively assembled panel wagon shows that the day of the low cost hot rod is still with us, and that its uses vary from being a fun car to one of functional value, haulin' everything from surfboards to... well, airplanes!

Little matter what active sport or hobby you choose to pursue, it seems there's always a bunch of gear to haul: surfboards, mini-bikes, parachutes, scuba tanks, skis, rock-hounding tools or telescopes. With Michael Ray it's big free-flight model planes, and the old question arose of how best to carry them. The obvious solution of a station wagon or pickup presented problems of high finance—but there's no holding down an old hot rodder, and when a fair little '28 Ford Sedan Delivery was spotted, the problems vanished. Even after 18 months of tinkering, Mike had added but $700 over the initial $200 paid for the panel, and now has an enviable hauler with under $1000 invested. Big step, of course, was to put in a V8, replacing the 4-banger. Tried and true, a '48 flathead was the low cost solution. For added plow, Ray installed a Winfield SU1A cam and adjustable lifters, Sharp 8:1 heads, Evans manifold with 2-2's and a Harman-Collins mag. The '39 Merc box couples to a '40 Ford rear end, with those hydraulic brakes and spindles added to the front as well. A '39 Nash steering just clears the exhaust headers tucked under a 3-piece 16-page steel hood. Mike and Gus Gordon painted the cherried body Roman Red acrylic when Gus and Don Henderson had finished with the metalwork. Art Tranafellow narrowed Citroen buckets 7 inches, completing the upholstery in black Naugahyde. Trying his hand at shows, Mike took first in Street Coupe/Sedans at the '65 Winternationals, and another 1st at the Los Angeles Surf Fair.

photography: LeRoi Smith

Sepulveda, California

Dave Kurz's car grabbed his eye when he saw it in the July 1965 *Hot Rod*.
Photo courtesy Hot Rod Magazine.

carb setup in 1965, it now runs a single early Ford four-barrel on an Edelbrock manifold.

The rear suspension uses coil-over shocks. There's a dropped front axle. Juice brakes from a 1940 Ford handle the stopping chores in front. The steering is still the 1939 Nash apparatus installed near vertical, Model-T style, by Michael Ray, lo those many years ago. Sixteen inch steel wheels are shod with 4.50 bias ply tires in front, 7.50s in back.

As a testament to Ray's craftsmanship, the car's doors and other panels fit as well as if the car had been built yesterday afternoon. There are no stress cracks in the paint, the doors shut solidly, and the hood aligns perfectly. Speaking of the hood, it is a three-piece affair punched on all three panels with rare round-top louvers (as opposed to the more common flat-topped style).

The interior is still the 40-year-old one, too, and it looks like new. The original paneling in the back has been painted gold. The narrowed Citroen bucket seats, modified and upholstered in black Naugahyde by Art Tranafellow sometime prior to 1965, are still in place and still look good.

Really about the only thing Dave has done to alter the outward appearance of the car is to add his studio logo to the side panels. Renowned pinstriper Alan Johnson handled that chore.

Dave's tale of his sedan delivery almost reads like a fairy tale romance, only the object of the affection in this case is four wheels and steel rather than flesh and blood. Still, the story has the right ending—and they lived happily ever after.

Wow, What a Pair of '39s! McMahan/Goodman
'39 Ford Tudors

Ask the average Randy Rodder or Reggie Restorer what his favorite fat-fendered Ford is. Almost to the man, the answer will be, "'40 Ford." Hardly anyone will mention the '39, yet the two are almost identical in most cases, at least in the overall silhouette and stance. Most body panels interchange between the two. Granted, the 1940 Deluxe grille is a design masterpiece. But the '39 Deluxe and '40 Standard grilles are nearly identical to each other and are lessons in

John McMahan's '39 Ford in profile.

simplicity. Their overall look is nearly the same as the '40 Deluxe and from a distance many folks cannot tell them apart, at least if they cannot see the grille.

Two Chattanooga, Tennessee, rodders have a pair of '39 sedans that illustrate how cool a '39 can be. One is a Standard and one is a Deluxe. Though both of the '39s here could be considered

traditional hot rods in the strictest sense, they are quite a bit different under the skin.

The Tucson Tan 1939 Ford Deluxe Tudor belongs to Mike Goodman. Mike is the president of the world famous Honest Charley Speed Shop in Chattanooga. Mike has been a hot rodder for most of his adult life and actually worked several years at the original Honest Charley shop with "Honest Hisself."

Mike Goodman's '39 Deluxe wears '40 Standard front sheetmetal.

This '39 Ford wears its 1940 Standard front end quite well.

Goodman's '39 Ford rod has a great profile, right or left.

Goodman's rod has a Halibrand axle center section.

His '39 is a bit of a rolling advertisement for the speed shop as it is a traditional hot rod, Honest's specialty, and it is equipped with quite a few goodies from the Honest Charley inventory of parts, along with some vintage pieces. It was built by Joe Smith of Joe Smith Early Ford in Marietta, Georgia, one of the better known rod builders in the Southeast.

The black 1939 Standard Tudor was built by another well-known hot rod builder, a specialist in Fords. Gene McKinney of Gene's Hot Rod Parts, just a few miles north of Chattanooga in Riceville, Tennessee, built that car for John McMahan. John is a Ford dealer and has his pick of any new Ford product to drive anytime. His favorite car? The '39, and rightly so. It's a sweetheart.

McMahan's looks closer to stock and has the fewest aftermarket parts and modifications. But some of its parts are very potent. The 1948 Mercury flathead is topped off with a Roadrunner

Engineering supercharger and two Stromberg 97 carbs. Suffice it to say, this little baby will run, and it sounds so sweet blasting through the dual straight pipes. There's not a sweeter gear head's lullaby than a flattie through straight pipes. It's like an angel singing.

The ignition on McMahan's Ford is a Mallory electronic for dependable spark. The suspension has reworked springs, tube shocks, and front and rear sway bars. Brakes are '40 Ford and the rearend is also a stock one with a 3.78 gear set. Yes, you guessed it. The car was set up as a moonshine runner. It is black, "all the better to *not* see you, my dear," built to run fast, handle well, and not draw undue attention. The interior is stock as well and has a banjo style wheel.

Most of the paint on John's car was applied in 1939. Yep, that's an original-paint car with the exception of a few small spray can touch-up spots. Ol' Henry had that black paint thing down pretty well.

In contrast to McMahan's stealth rod, Mike Goodman's '39 has tons of aftermarket speed equipment on it (but no supercharger). Induction on its 1949 Ford truck flathead engine is handled by a pair of the ubiquitous Stromberg 97s on an Edelbrock manifold. Ported and relieved Navarro heads cover Ross pistons wrapped in Grant rings and Chevy six cylinder valves. An Isky 1007 cam opens said valves. The engine was built by Bradley Dennis and Joe Smith, about as good a pair of engine builders as you'll find.

One of the most recognizable profiles in all of motordom.

McMahan's interior is dark and stealthy; Goodman's is light.

The '40 Standard grille was similar to the '39 Deluxe but lights and hood differ.

The beauty of sedans is the big ol' back seat.

The suspension is the most updated, wearing the most modern parts. Posie springs are used at both ends. The front is buggy-style and rears are leafs. There are front and rear Chassis Engineering sway bars, a Super Bell four-inch dropped front axle and spindles, as well as Pete & Jake's shocks and disc brakes. Steering is through a stock '39 column, but with a Vega cross steer arrangement. Mike hangs on to a banjo wheel while he's steering this baby. The rear end is a coveted Halibrand quick-change center with 9-inch Ford axles.

Anyone who shuns a '39 Ford to pay more money for a '40 needs to spend a few minutes looking these two jewels over. They are about as close to the definition of "hot rod" as any car with windows and a steel top can get. Such a deal.

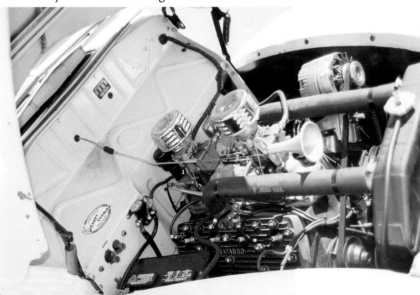

Navarro heads, Edelbrock manifold, Stromberg 97s in Goodman's car.

The '40 Ford headlights and sheetmetal on Mike's '39 confuse the masses.

The infamous and desirable Ford banjo wheel.

McMahan's '39 Ford Standard has teardrop headlights and a prowed front end .

Open wide and say, "Moonshine."

The Roadrunner blower on McMahan's '39 makes power instantly and always.

Racer's Roaring Roadster—
Jackie Howerton's

1932 Ford Roadster

Racing and rodding—the more you delve into the history aspects of hot rodding, the stronger the connection appears. Racers and rodders are cut from the same cloth, even racers who don't have hot rods and hot rodders who don't race. It's like two groups of people in the same big open field, separated only by a chalk line in the grass. The line could disappear with two minutes of rain. It could be crossed with one step in either direction.

Jackie Howerton walks back and forth across that line like it's not even there. He's been involved in both and sometimes he's in both worlds on the same day…or the same hour.

He comes by it honestly. His dad was a professional race car driver in their native Oklahoma. Jackie started out driving modifieds in the area surrounding Tulsa, Oklahoma. Later he moved to Indianapolis, which was still considered in the late 1960s and into the 1970s as the mecca for his type of racing. Actually to many people it still is. He raced full-time for awhile until the pressures of family life (a wife and three kids expecting to eat every day) drove him to take a regular job and do the racing thing on the side.

Howerton spent some time working for the Patrick and Bignotti racing teams. Finally he opened his own shop, Howerton Racing Products, first in his

The '32 Ford roadster in a quiet, peaceful setting.

Without fenders, parts of the suspension and tie rods show.

The rear of Howerton's roadster has the hot rod favorite '39 Ford lights.

garage, and then he moved to a new location on Gasoline Alley, just a few blocks south of the Indianapolis Motor Speedway. One of the shop's specialties was repairing crashed Indy cars. It also built a stock-block car for racer Gary Irvin. The shop currently provides custom racing headers to many NASCAR and Indy Car teams.

If the Howerton name sounds familiar, though, it might be due to one of Jackie's better known races in a USAC Champ Car. Bob Jennings describes it well in his Bob Jennings' World of Racing account.

"Teamed with Al Unser in the powerful Vel's Parnelli Jones stable, Mario (Andretti) ended his stellar dirt track career at the Hoosier Hundred on the Indiana State Fairgrounds mile on September 7, 1974. He started the race and checkered third behind winner Jackie Howerton and Unser in the closest three-car Hoosier Hundred finish in history. The 1974 Hoosier Hundred was a dandy.

"Today Jackie Howerton is known as a master fabricator in local racing circles. He has a shop on Rowena Street (better known as Gasoline Alley) about one mile directly south of the Indianapolis Motor Speedway. Howerton is one of the more prominent subcontractors in the racing cottage industry that exists in Indianapolis. In 1974 he was a USAC race driver. He was in a car entered by Andy Granatelli

and STP which was powered by a turbocharged Offy.

"I don't recall exactly what Granatelli's role in the Howerton entry was. By 1974 he was no longer running an Indy car team but was still directly involved in the marketing efforts of STP. Perhaps it was the challenge of trying to make a turbo Offy work on the dirt. The turbo Offy was the Indy car engine of choice at that time. Actually it was the only Indy car power you could buy in those days, since A.J. Foyt wasn't selling the Foyt V-8 after he bought the Ford Motor Company Indy car inventory in 1971. The old Ford DOHC V-8 had become the popular engine in USAC dirt car competition. Both Unser and

Original dash was reworked for Auburn gauges. Wheel is real Bell Racing sprint.

Open roadster doors show off the roadster's interior.

Black exhaust headers and frame contrast the bright red engine.

Top to bottom: Stromberg, Eddie Meyer, Evans, Fenton.

Halibrand quick change rearend, Model A spring.

Andretti were running the Ford V-8 in their Viceroy dirt cars.

"I think Howerton qualified on pole. What I do remember was that Howerton had just enough extra power to hold off Al and Mario. Lap after lap, Howerton's dayglow red STP car led the two Viceroy cars out of turn four and past our seats at the west end

Nick Alexander owned the car for awhile; Ben's his dad.

Only one Hallock windshield exists for '32 Fords. Here it is.

of the main straightaway. I kept hoping that Unser could find a way past Jackie but he wasn't able, try as he might." – Bob Jennings (www.bjwor.com)

Oddly enough, Howerton didn't build this particular '32 Ford roadster, though he does have a couple of other awesome cars under construction at his home shop. This car was owned by Joe Mac from Ford Parts Obsolete for 35 years. It has been a hot rod since at least the 1940s and Jackie has an old photo of it with a Cadillac grille shell at that time.

The owner of the car previous to Jackie was Nick Alexander, son of the late actor Ben Alexander, one of the stars of the original *Dragnet* TV

series. Ben owned a Ford dealership in San Francisco at one time and a die cast license frame from the dealership is still on this car.

This roadster is definitely one that would appeal to a race car guy. The '46 Mercury flathead is running a 3 3/8-inch bore and a 4 1/8-inch stroke. That computes to 296 cubes. Dual Strombergs sit atop a tall, polished Eddie Meyer manifold. It also uses a Potvin cam and has Evans heads. Ignition system is a Harmon Collins design. Fenton cast iron headers and dual Smithys sing the sweet flathead song. The 1939 Ford transmission is stuffed with Lincoln Zephyr gears, as was the practice in the 1940s and 1950s.

There is a Halibrand quick change rear end, suspended off a Model A spring. Brakes are from a '48 Ford and the wheels are triple pinstriped 16-inch steel versions with 5.25-inch front tires, and 7.00-inch at the rear.

The roadster wears primer applied by the Kennedy Boys and an extremely rare windshield from the hands of Duke Hallock. Hallock made several Model A roadster windshields and they were reportedly cast in a high school shop foundry. Only one was ever made for a Deuce and this is it.

Howerton's '32 has a reworked Deuce dash filled with actual Auburn gauges. It also has an original Bell Racing steering wheel sitting on the F-100 column. The seats are upholstered in brown leather.

Jackie Howerton's roadster is one of those cars with a special appeal. It looks like it's not quite finished, but it is. It runs great, handles like a champ and sounds, oh, so good running through those Smithys. Mmmmm, yes.

The famed Eddie Meyer logo.

The AAA was the sanctioning body for the Indy 500 through 1955.

SECTION 3

New Old School

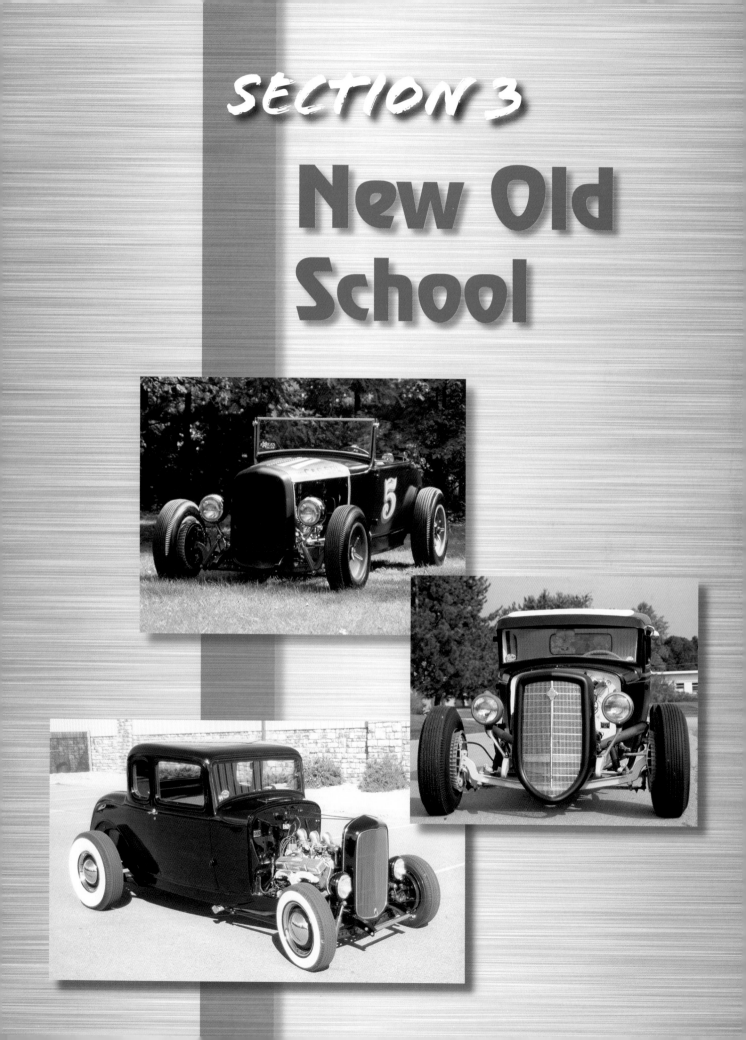

Roy Caruthers'

1931 Ford Roadster

It's no secret that early hot rodders were also racers. The lines between early street hot rods and their racing counterparts were fuzzy at best. Usually they were invisible because the cars were the same ones. The guys would drive the cars to work all week, wrench on them in the evening, and take them to the tracks on the weekend.

Roy Caruthers' 1931 Ford roadster, a relatively recent build, falls in that mold. Roy makes his living as a UPS semi driver, but is a former racer and comes from a family of racers around the Indianapolis area.

His racing connections date back to the days when many of the Indy 500 racers actually lived in and around Indianapolis. Their cars were locally built and sponsored, and the guys hung out at each other's shops and garages. They raced USAC midgets and sprints against each other on Midwest dirt tracks and were literally the gearhead next door.

In other words, we're talking about the days before big money came to racing—when an Indy car might only have a half-dozen sponsor decals on it, and the pit uniforms consisted of work pants and T-shirts. Many members of the pit crews were volunteers from the owner's or driver's circle

The 1931 Ford roadster shows its "going away" stance.

The rear wheels are off AJ. Foyt's 1962 Indianapolis 500 car.

Taillights are junkyard finds from an unknown vintage Chrysler product.

of friends. They worked evenings and weekends cranking out race car parts and hot rod parts on actual hand-cranked Bridgeport milling machines and LeBlond lathes. They might assemble most of the car in the yard out behind the shop because the actual shop was full of customers' cars.

Roy and his friends still hang out around Gasoline Alley, the light industrial area just a few blocks from the famed Brickyard. Several of those guys still work in racing-related businesses there and it doesn't take too much imagination to look around that part of Indianapolis and the actual suburb named Speedway and imagine what it was like there 40 or 50 years ago.

Indianapolis was a town where it wasn't unusual to walk into a White Castle burger joint and bump into a Foyt, an Andretti or Unser, Rodger Ward, Joe Leonard, or a relative of Wilbur Shaw. The Granatelli brothers were like Indy's favorite sons.

Roy's dad was a dry lakes racer at one time and Dad's car was actually pictured in the very first issue of *Hot Rod Magazine*. Art Chrisman later owned and modified the car, setting several records with it. It now resides in the Wally Parks NHRA Museum in California. Roy is in the process of building a replica of the car as it was when his dad owned it.

The '31 that Roy is driving now has some racing connections of its own, at least in its componentry. The Winters quick-change rear end center section is

The nose view shows a mix of old and very old.

1953 DeSoto instrument cluster is attached to a hand-formed dashboard.

Clean and basic rod accoutrements, the upholstery came from Mexico.

Few hot rod roadsters would look better than this 1931 Ford.

The Foyt wheels and Ralph's exhausts give this Ford roadster a definite Indy flavor.

Headers are homemade and connect to a Ralph's Muffler

The 1949 Ford Flathead has an Offy intake with three

The "Flattie" has all the right stuff including a Schneider cam and Offy heads.

from the last midget racecar that Roy owned. Andy Hurtebise, son of the late, legendary Indy driver, Jim Hurtebise, helped Roy with the machine work to get the quick-change, sprint car hubs and real knock-offs to mate to 8-inch Ford axles and '40 Ford axle housings.

The rear 18-inch Halibrand Indy car wheels were actually on A.J. Foyt's 1962 Indianapolis 500 car. The left one fell off his car right after a pit stop and very possibly cost him the race win. Pity the man who failed to tighten that knock-off!

By the way, Roy traded a weed eater for that wheel! You can't get much more old school than swapping for parts. It's the American way!

Roy has fashioned his car to look exactly like the period hot rods of the 1950s and he's done a masterful job of it. Other than the all but invisible five-speed transmission and cut down seat, both out of an S-10 pickup, the newest known components are the '62 Indy car wheels.

The dash center section is from a 1953 DeSoto. It resides on a dashboard that Roy and friend Tom Culbertson formed over an oxygen bottle. The taillights are from some unidentified Chrysler in a junkyard.

Roy has a strong love for hot rods and he has a thing for hot rodding, too. Knowing what looks right on a hot rod, how the overall car should look, and where to get the pieces he needs are all second nature to this Indy rodder, a founding member of the Exiles Car Club. One could say that Roy is connected, but in a good way. He knows people who do things the old school way from several different aspects. These guys hand form their own sheetmetal. They cut and weld their own frames, they make things that aren't supposed to work together actually work together.

Denny Jamison was involved in the creation of the louvered hood. Denny, who owns Hammer

Authentic Indy car knock-offs were adapted by Andy Hurtebise.

Art Automotive in Indianapolis, also applied the black paint to the car. The numbers and lettering "5" and "C&C Special" came from the talented hands of Dan Shaw.

Power for the C&C Special is courtesy of a 1949 Ford Flattie. It wears an original vintage Offenhauser manifold and three Stromberg 97 carburetors. Ignition is Mallory and headers are homemade. The Schneider cam and Ross pistons are icing on the Flathead speed equipment who's-who cake.

For a local historical link, Ralph's Muffler Shop was reportedly Indy's first speed shop. They are still in business and they did the exhaust system on Roy's '31. Seems only fitting, doesn't it?

Front brake backing plates are from a '40 Ford, hand cut with a torch to resemble a set that Roy spotted in the Indianapolis Motor Speedway Museum. Brake shoes were drilled to complete the look.

Front wheels are vintage 16-inch Halibrands carrying 6.00 tires, while the rear Halibrands

Brakes and shocks are definitely not Ford original equipment!

wear 7.00 x 18 tires. Springs are leaf, of course, and the seat upholstery is from a Mexican blanket.

This car could easily pass for a vintage build; it's that good. Many a hot rod enthusiast has mistaken it for a survivor car built long ago. It is a perfect example of timeless hot rod styling and the utilization of proper componentry that all works together perfectly to give the look that its owner was seeking.

Front wheels are rare genuine Halibrand racing solids.

Neal East's "1 LOST 1932"

Ford Three-Window Coupe

Is this the perfect Deuce coupe hot rod? If not, it comes very, very close. Neal East is the current lucky man to own this car, but he'll also be the first to tell you that *all* the credit for it goes to Don Coleman. Neal's proud of the car, but he's humble enough to give credit where credit is due, and there's a lot due here for sure.

By the way, yes, *that* Neal East, formerly and repeatedly of *Rod & Custom* fame, former owner of

Neal East's Don Coleman-built '32 might just be the perfect Deuce 5-window.

the Doane Spencer roadster, etc. He knows his hot rods, OK, and he *might* have had a hand in building and/ or resurrecting a couple. These days Neal owns a wonderful automotive bookstore called Colorado Car Books in Littleton, Colorado, just outside Denver.

The face that has launched a million hot rod dreams.

The three-window Ford has a classic hot rod stance.

The Ford's front end is simple, yet has artistic lines.

Even the Ford V-8 badge was well designed.

Don Coleman found this car's body in the woods and built on that foundation. A very talented gent, he did it all—chassis, brakes, paint, upholstery, top chop, everything. Each of those different parts of the car is perfect and he did them all. A few guys got all the talent.

Check the reflections in the black paint on this ebony jewel. It takes a very smooth body to wear black paint and not be ashamed to be seen in public. This gal has the bod for it. Even in the bright sun, there's not a flaw.

Left and right front views show off this special Ford hot rod.

The filled original dash is now filled with eight of Stewart-Warner's finest.

Don Coleman – a man of many talents - stitched the interior, too.

Coleman upholstered the trunk in the black and white as the interior.

"Coleman " nameplate is from an old Denver-based truck company.

The top is chopped three inches, a number that is just about right in most cases. Famed customizer Gene Winfield says, "If you're not gonna chop it at least three inches, don't bother to chop it at all." Three was the right choice here, Gene.

Neal's '32 is powered by the requisite Ford flathead, this particular one from a 1948 Mercury. It blows out through headers and dual Smithy's mufflers. Edelbrock heads match Edelbrock intake manifold and Strombergs. The transmission of power to the rear wheels is the responsibility of the tried and true '39 Ford gearbox.

The front brakes from a Ford F-150 pickup provide excellent stopping power and they are mounted inside the desirable Buick finned aluminum brake drums. The rear end is out of a 1936 Ford, while the front end is a combination of a dropped beam axle and tubular shocks.

The interior that Don Coleman stitched together for this coupe is almost as pretty as the outside. Black and white tuck and roll Naugahyde covering the original '32 bench seat looks great with the black body. The door hardware was liberated from a 1949 Ford. A 1956 Ford truck

The '48 Merc flattie has Edelbrock heads and manifold.

donated its steering column, as so many have over the years. This one even had turn signals. A '39 Ford banjo wheel gives Neal something to hold on to when he's motoring around Denver area streets. The dashboard is a filled '32 panel with eight Stewart-Warner gauges. Vintage rock and roll must surely emanate from the radio under the dash.

The very rare and unusual "Colorado Lost" license plate with the number 1932 is actually registered to this car. What were the chances of finding something like that, one in a bazillion?

That Coleman nameplate mounted on the rear spreader bar was originally on a Denver-built Coleman truck. Coleman built heavy-duty trucks, airport tractors, and four-wheel drive conversions for many decades in Denver. Neal leaves the nameplate on there for a couple of reasons, but foremost is to pay homage to the gent who built his beautiful coupe.

A black car must be smoooooth to earn the color. This one is.

CH18

"Chef's Tudor"— Denver Richardson's '29 Ford Tudor

The hot rod gene is definitely passed from one generation to the next, and it's a beautiful thing. The Marietta, Georgia, Richardson family certainly proves that. Both father Mark and son Denver are into hot rodding up to their eyeballs. Denver and Mark are members of the Atlanta Road Kings car club and both dig and drive traditional hot rods.

The term rat rod has come into vogue in recent years, and it's used to describe all kinds of dissimilar cars that appear out of the ordinary to non-rodders. Denver's

1929 Ford Model A Tudor sedan might appear to fit that mostly undefined genre to the casual, uninitiated observer. Such an observation would be totally incorrect. There is nothing rat-like about this car. It is extremely well built, it is safe, and it runs like the proverbial scalded dog. *A.S.P.C.A. disclaimer: no dogs were actually scalded in making this comparison. It's only a figure of speech.*

Looking at Denver's car makes one wonder why there aren't more Model A sedan rods being built. Most people tend to gravitate toward the coupes, but the sedan makes a great hot rod, and there are many more sedans available than coupes. The sedan is especially good for a taller person, because it allows for a more rearward placement of the driver's seat, thus allowing more legroom. Legroom is at a premium in Model A coupes. Keep in mind that the average person was not as tall in 1929 as today. Cars were sized accordingly.

The SBC makes this lightweight Tudor a smooth highway runner.

Guide 682-C headlights look good on any early rod, this one included.

Filled cowl and more Top Hat artistry.

Henry Ford thought the perfect sized car was one that fit *him*, and he was a shorty.

Denver and his dad, Mark, built this car and it has been both chopped and channeled three inches. Dropping things a little further is a four-inch dropped I-beam front axle with hairpins and a custom crossmember. That accounts for a height adjustment of 10 inches right off the top...well, the top and the bottom...and the middle. Add (or subtract) the difference in tire height between the original tall skinnies and the current 165/75-15s and 265/75-15s and you can see why the car sits so much lower than a stock Model A.

Denver painted the car himself—with rattle cans—lots of rattle cans. His index finger is still cramping. Then he had Top Hat pinstripe the body and dashboard in white. You'll notice

Stock visor was drilled for effect.

The checkered flag firewall stands out.

Denver Richardson even has a city named after him!

that except for a few accents in red (such as the wheels and front axle), the entire car follows a black and white theme. That extends to a white top insert and the black and white checkered firewall, too.

The Model A sun visor was drilled for effect. The headlights on Denver's sedan are the ever-popular Guide 682-C models with integral parking lights/turn signals. Taillights are aftermarket '39 Ford teardrops with the devil lenses. The fuel tank has been moved from the cowl to the rear. That allowed for more legroom inside and for the firewall to be recessed outside.

The firewall recess allowed ample room for the mostly stock Chevy 305 and TurboHydramatic 350. Mallory provided the ignition system and the induction system is all Edelbrock. The tube headers feed into a custom exhaust system bent 'n' built by James at Cherokee Tire.

Champion ribbed insert adorns the stock dashboard.

"Chef's Tudor"— Denver Richardson's '29 Ford Tudor

The rear stance of the "Chef's Tudor" is unique.

Pinstriping was done by Top Hat.

Fuel tank was moved to the rear from the cowl area.

Brad Shore upholstery covers owner-built seats.

The white steering wheel brings out the white trim accents.

The cockpit of Denver's hot rod features seats that he built with his own two hands. Brad Shore did the upholstery in black with white piping. The stock dash is accentuated with a Champion finned insert. A white-rimmed (what else?) steering wheel is bolted to the Lime Works column. New windows by Wild Bill at A&S Glass keep the elements at bay.

Denver Richardson is a professional chef by day. If his dishes are as tasty as his hot rod, he should do very well.

Coilovers and ladder bars keep the 8-inch Ford axle in check.

Exhaust includes the option of cutouts.

CH19

"Rockabilly '32"—
Dennis Brackeen's

'32 Ford Three-Window Coupe

This car is a fooler. More than one seasoned hot rod guy has looked Dennis Brackeen's '32 five-window over pretty closely and assumed it was built in the 1950s or 1960s. "Period correct" is not a term to be thrown around lightly because it is much overused, but Dennis' car fits it. Looks can be deceiving; it was built less than four years ago.

Dennis Brackeen is a *huge* fan of rockabilly music, which is the music of choice among most traditional hot rodders. That's because it was the popular music of the day during the original heyday of hot rodding, the mid-1950s to very early 1960s. Dennis knows many of the old rockers and most of the modern-day ones. His cool coupe fits right in with that whole scene, man.

He also has an affinity for Fender Stratocaster guitars and

Looking like it was made for a 1950s car magazine, this hot rod is just a few years old.

Stock '32 Ford dash has an engine-turned insert.

This is a '32 Ford that enjoys Corvette power!

Tasteful black and white tuck and roll upholstery.

Ventilation is available from a tip-out windshield – it's 1932 A/C!

This Ford is photogenic from any angle chosen.

A tiny Wynn's Friction Proofing sticker means this Ford's engine runs smoothly.

The eyes of Moon are upon you!

Classic looks – a '32 Deuce 5-window highboy – can't be beat.

The lowered front end of the "Rockabilly" '32 Ford coupe.

other objects de rock 'n' roll. He has donated memorabilia to the Rockabilly Hall of Fame in Jackson, Tennessee.

One of the fooling features on Dennis' rod is the paint of the window garnish moldings. It's orange and a little scratched-up. Apparently the car was orange in an earlier life. The decision to leave them as is was a wise one because they add to the flavor of the car immensely. The rest of the interior is a beautiful, tasteful tuck and roll in black and white. The steering column is out of a 1940 Ford.

Motivation comes courtesy of a Corvette 350 engine topped with an Edelbrock tri-power manifold, but with Carter carburetors rather than the more common Holleys or Rochesters. Curved velocity stacks keep cats and large birds from getting sucked in. Ram's horn exhaust manifolds give a nostalgic flavor. Delco handles the ignition as it has since the engine was a baby. A tried-and-true Turbo 350 transmission is used as well as an equally proven Ford 9-inch rear.

A deuce highboy just looks best with bias-ply whitewalls and Dennis followed that basic axiom. The big-and-little versions are 8.90 x 15 and 5.60 x 15, just as God intended.

Classic bullet-shaped 1937 Ford taillights with blue dots are utilized on the rear frame rails. The car's brakes are the well-proven 1940 Ford versions (can there be a '40 Ford left anywhere with its brakes?).

Dennis Brackeen makes up half of the casual racing team of Brackeen & Longwell Racing, along with his old pal Warren Longwell. Obviously Dennis appreciates fine machinery and knows how to build it, too.

It's a Ford rear end handling the Chevy's power.

1937 Ford blue-dots light the back way.

The "Rockabilly" Ford shows off its memorable profile.

The Shop Truck— Josh Mills'

1933 Ford truck

Josh Mills has to have one of the coolest jobs in the world of gearheads. He is part owner and chief fabricator at Joe Smith Ford & Street Rod Parts in Marietta, Georgia. The place is basically Mecca for all things Ford hot rod or resto on the north side of Atlanta. He is also a founding member of the Atlanta Road Kings car club. Josh builds hot rods and cool motorcycles by day for pay, and then by night he builds hot rods and cool motorcycles for himself. He built this 1933 Ford pick-up a few years ago and it has been his daily driver ever since.

The '33 was no virgin to the torch when Josh got it. The truck had been hot-rodded to the hilt in the 1950s, and drag raced at some time, too. But it had fallen into disrepair in later years. That earlier molestation had taken the form of a reasonable 3-1/2 inch top chop, but also a radical nine inches of channeling. That's quite a bit for a driver over, say three feet tall! So Josh and Hank Young

It's all about the proportions so they must be right.

unchanneled it a bit to a more reasonable five inches or so. That way, Josh could have seats and not sit on the floor with his legs folded in front of him. That's a much better arrangement for a vehicle intended as a daily driver, don't you agree?

The cab was also moved back about four inches. There was a considerable amount of rot in the trucks panels, so Josh and Hank replaced a few inches-worth all the way around and modified the firewall a bit for the engine of choice while they were at it.

Most '33 Ford trucks don't look like this version!

Thirty-six louvers let the truck bed breathe.

The winged radiator cap tops the famous Ford blue oval logo (inset).

A Buick V-8 keeps this Ford in motion.

The right look for hot rods is based a lot on proportions. With the chopped and channeled cab massaged to a better look, the truck's bed was way too long. It was determined to be precisely 9-½ inches too long, so that much was exorcised. While the bed was apart anyway, it was a good time to punch six rows of six louvers in the tailgate. A 1932 commercial grille shell completes "the look."

While tooling to work one day in his previous vehicle, Josh happened to spot a '59 Buick with a 401 Nailhead engine for sale. Within a few minutes, the motor became his own. He rebuilt it and added some very slightly oversized pistons, taking the displacement to a real fine 409. Ported and polished 1964 Buick heads were used. The Buford runs unencumbered by such things as hoods, so clearance was no problem for the Offenhauser manifold/Holley carb tri-power set-up. The big ol' Buick valves are operated by a vintage Schneider camshaft. Homemade 1936 Ford torque tube headers are sometimes open, sometimes closed, depending on the mood and the neighborhoods to be traversed.

Josh pressed a 1955 Pontiac generator into service. A Ronco magneto supplies spark for the Buick. The heads are dressed in 1956 valve covers. An M22 "Rock Crusher" 4-speed sits behind the Nailhead. It gets stirred around quite often in the suburban Atlanta traffic.

A nine-inch rear end out of a 1957 Ford station wagon was utilized in back. It's attached to a custom crossmember via a '37 Ford trailing arm. The front axle is a drilled and dropped I-beam located by '46 split wishbones. Bias ply tires on steel wheels are the only way to go on a truck like this one, so that was the combo of choice. Front Firestones are 4.75 x 16 while the rears are 7.00 x 16.

With the power train and body needs addressed, Josh was ready to move on to the interior, his rolling office of sorts. Genuine B-17 bomber seats were acquired from an Alabama airplane graveyard, and then Josh stitched up some black rolled and pleated covers to make them comfy. Aviation seatbelts complete that look. The dashboard is the

The 1959 Buick Nailhead now displaces 409 cubes.

Door hardware was once in a 1950 Ford.

The business office has a '33 dash with vintage S-W gauges.

stock '33 Ford unit with a few 1950s Stewart Warner black-faced gauges in the middle. The steering wheel is a 1940 Ford hoop. The steering box came from a '39 pickup. The shifter came out of another 1939 Ford. The tachometer mounted under the dash is an actual Westach from 1951. Door handles and window cranks were once in a 1950 Ford.

Did you notice that Josh Mills is a bit of a purist when it comes to early hot rods? New parts,

Headers were fashioned from '36 torque tubes.

They're genyoowine B-17 bomber seats.

we don't need no stinkin' new parts! Josh's truck is an excellent example of some of the newer-built hot rods that defy the casual observer's attempts to date the build. This truck could have been built in 1959 or 1964 or 2002. Can't tell by looking. It's a timeless style and it uses timeless components.

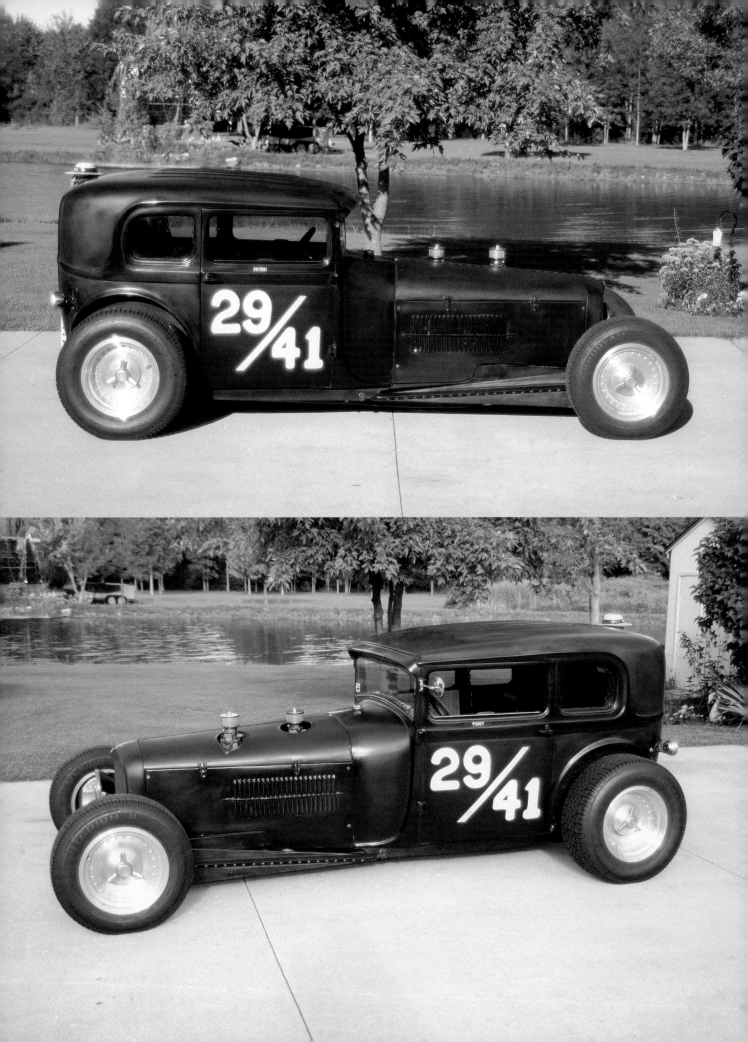

Tony Messina's "Hard Times"
1929 Ford Tudor

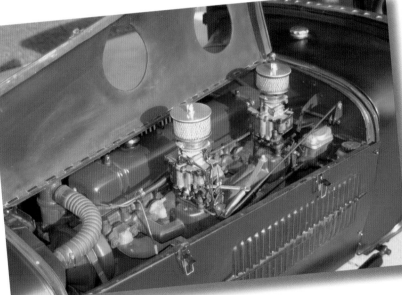

The long 1941 Buick straight-8 engine.

Tony Messina's 1929 Ford Tudor was one of the hits of the Detroit Autorama. It is so radical, yet simple and practical, that the gear heads just kept looking it over and over from every angle. What's even more amazing about this car is the dollar investment. Tony claims he has $4000 in this car. That's it. Have you ever seen such a cool rod for $4000, at least in modern times? No, you haven't.

The car has several whimsical touches, too, and talking to Tony, it soon becomes apparent that he takes neither himself nor his hot rod too seriously. Hot rodding is fun, and there it shall remain.

Look this car's photos over closely and you'll see that it has been severely modified. It also has a ton of ingenious homebuilt touches. Many of the major mods were done to accommodate the engine of choice, a 1941 straight-eight Buick. That sucker is looooong! It definitely required some surgery to fit it into a car originally equipped with a four banger.

Tony started by whacking a full 20 inches out of the body length, mostly in the quarter window vicinity. He basically took a Tudor sedan body and made a long coupe out of it. While he had the Sawzall in hand, he also chopped the top four inches. Then Tony stretched the car in the engine-bay area by 14 inches. The result is a car that looks very little

Watts link serves to keep the axle aligned properly.

How low can you go? Pretty darned low!

The long hood covers the long Buick's engine.

like its former self. The main body has somewhat of a resemblance to an Austin Bantam but with a long—very long—nose. After all the corrective surgery, the body was finished off with Rustoleum paint and sanded with a Scotch-Brite pad for the desired sheen.

As expected, no one makes an off-the-shelf hood for this particular set-up, so Tony made his own with scallops and flares around the air cleaner holes. "Made

his own" will be a recurring theme in this story. His Fair Haven, Michigan, garage has turned out several cool hot rods. This one is just the latest.

The 1941 Buick straight eight is mostly stock except for the air cleaners. That huge torque monster came with dual Stromberg carburetors from the factory. It has dual exhaust running through straight pipes and exiting fishtail-style in Tony's homemade

Push bars, exhaust tips, and louvered panel all wear the homemade brand.

The "29/41" signifies Hard Times.

Blue Plexiglas windows are ¼-inch thick.

11-inch tips. A straight eight Buick blowing through straight pipes is like a symphony. The transmission is a Saginaw four-speed.

The suspension is another area of interest on this very interesting hot rod. All four corners have independently-operated air bags. The front dropped tube axle is located by a Watts link. It keeps the front axle oriented correctly and serves as a conversation starter as well. Trivia bonus: Scottish inventor James Watt devised the Watts link in the 18th century! The rear end is from a 327

Front brake scoops used to be an aluminum saucepan.

1941 Buick straight eight is a stocker.

Tony couldn't even leave the key alone. It's been customized, too.

Tony Messina is a member of the Roadents Car Club.

Camaro and has a single traction bar.

Tony's car has disc brakes all around. The front ones are cooled by scoops that were made by cutting an aluminum saucepan in half. Want some more homemade? Check the louvers in the rear pan behind the *homemade* rear push bars. Those were in panels of some old electrical boxes that Tony had

lying around. He cut those out and formed them to fit in his rolled pan.

Want more? The vertical bars in the chopped '32 Ford grille shell were made from the wire out of real estate signs. Ingenious!

The interior has a bunch more Tony Messina touches. That swoopy polished aluminum panel above the instrument panel was

The interior has lots of custom touches.

one of his fabrications. He couldn't even leave the ignition key alone! He customized the head of it, too, with holes and ribs. The seats are fiberglass race car seats from Speedway Motors and they have Speedway's black vinyl upholstery on them.

The console is from a 1964 Chevy Impala SS four-speed car. In describing the "headliner," Tony says it consists of "…wooden slats made to look like a woody, sort of." The steering column was "made from parts" and hooks to a rack and pinion. Windows are cut from ¼-inch blue Plexiglas. There are window frames made of welded chain. Lights in the eyes of the "Hard Times" skull in the

rear function as the high-mounted stoplight.

Tony describes his rationale for naming the car hard times and explains the 29/41 numbers on the side.

"The 29/41 on the doors is significant for the Hard Times on the skull's hat. 1929 was the year of the car body and also was the year of the great stock market crash. The 41 is the year of the straight eight motor by Buick, and also the year of the attack on Pearl Harbor. Thus, the name Hard Times."

Well, the name may be Hard Times, but the car has definitely contributed to some good times.

Inside is a '64 Impala SS 4-speed console.

Johnnie Walker Green Label

'32 Ford Five-Window Coupe

This car is slick, having been built by one of the top rod building shops in the country, Dave Crouse's Custom Auto in Loveland, Colorado. But it is certainly not a trailer queen or garage flower. It gets driven a lot of miles. As a testament to its build quality, it has been trouble-free. That's always a good trait for a driver!

Gunnison, Colorado, owner Johnnie Walker is a plumber by trade, so he knows the value of having a professional do the job he's most qualified for. That's why he and wife Laura had Custom

Auto build the car while he spent his time laying pipe to pay for it.

One major thing that sets this car apart from the rest of the Deuce coupe pack is its Hemi engine. Yep, it's a *real* Hemi from Chrysler's heyday. This particular one came from a 1954 Chrysler. It's one of the 331-cubic inch variety and it's backed up by a

more contemporary Richmond five-speed manual gearbox.

The engine has an Edmunds 2 x 4 intake manifold with a pair of Carter WCFB carbs. Mallory ignition sets the gas mixture aflame. Those valve covers are ultra-rare Parker cast aluminum. Johnnie found a pair of the unfinished castings and had them machined to finish proportions. Original Hemi truck exhaust manifolds take spent gasses away to a custom exhaust system.

It looks like a '32 Ford but this one has a real Hemi kick to it!

The upholstery is green leather over a Rod Tin repop seat.

Apple green pinstripes on dark green paint, and perfect panel alignment.

Vintgage Ford interior includes a Ford truck steering wheel and column plus a recent floor-mounted shifter.

Trunk got the gray vinyl treatment.

The interior of Walker's Deuce is especially inviting. Its green leather seat is a reproduction version of the original by Rod Tin. Contrasting gray vinyl door panels were used to match the gray carpet. The trunk got the same gray treatment. The dashboard is an original '32 with a Stewart-Warner Ensign gauge panel. A 1958 Ford truck steering column was used and 1948 Ford door handles and window

The 1954 Hemi has rare Parker aluminum valve covers.
Photo courtesy Roger Jetter

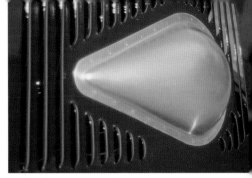

Hand-formed bubbles clear the Hemi.

Guide 682-C lights are mounted on the original '32 bar.

The Ford's hood is open revealing the 1954 Hemi engine.

Front I-beam is drilled and chromed.

cranks set things off with a little shininess.

Outside, the bodywork is flawless. The top was chopped three inches, and then everything was given the smooth-over. It was then painted DuPont dark green by Dustin Weir. Pinstripes are apple green. Taillights are round 1950 Pontiac units. Those aluminum hood blisters were necessary to clear the Hemi's valve covers. They were hand-hammered over wooden bucks by Rex Rodgers. Those Custom Auto chaps do good work.

Guide 682-C headlights are mounted on the stock Ford headlight bar. The license plate light is a period aftermarket Hollywood light and the license frame is a Ford accessory.

The chassis of the Johnnie Walker car is built for eating up the miles. The 1959 9-inch Ford rear end is hung on coilover shocks. Gear ratio is 3.50 to 1. Remember the five-speed. It has an overdrive so cruising is at a relatively low RPM. The front end has a dropped I-beam with hairpins. The rear wheels are magnesium Halibrands shod with 7.00 x 16 tires. Front wheels are the same style Vintiques with 5.60 x 15 rubber.

What else can be said? One of Henry's most beautiful designs has been taken a few steps further and turned into a comfortable, traditional highway eater. You're a lucky man, Johnnie Walker, a lucky man indeed.

CH 23

A Hot Rod Builder's Hot Rod— Tom Culbertson's

1930 Ford Coupe

Tom Culbertson knows a thing or three about building hot rods. He's been doing it professionally since 1965 when he got home to Indianapolis from the Marines. He builds cars that are driven and his own 1930 Model A coupe is certainly no exception to that rule.

When asked to start it up, Tom responds, "Well, it's been sitting a couple weeks, it might not start." Then he climbs behind the wheel, turns the key and it fires right up. This car has been driven to Las Vegas and to California (separate trips), to Florida, and Chicago and to the Northeast, as well as all over the Midwest. It is an ultra-dependable driver.

Bias-ply whitewalls on chrome wheels lookin' good.

Tom's coupe used to run the usual '32 filled grille shell. No more. He was at a swap meet a couple of years ago and picked up a very rare Indiana truck grille shell. The Indiana trucks were built by White Motors (see the similarity now?) for only a few years at their plant in Indiana. They were basically a White with a few small differences. Anyway,

Tom liked the looks of the grille shell, so he sectioned it, narrowed it and made it look like it belongs on his Indiana hot rod.

The coupe has been sectioned a little and chopped a little, then finished out in PPG satin black by Brian Whiteis. The top panel is starkly contrasting white. The taillights are from a '51 Oldsmobile.

Underneath is some pretty cool stuff, including the 9-inch Ford rear end that was painted light green like the rest of the

The black 1930 Ford coupe is set off by whitewalls and a white inert on top.

Culbertson pinstriped the rear axle. Not much room to work under there.

A set of these art deco lights sold on eBay for over $1,800 recently.

chassis, then pinstriped by Tom, presumably *before* it went under the car. He's an accomplished pinstriper and has been for a long time. Many of the pinstriped cars in the Midwest, and especially hot rods around Indianapolis, have had their lines pulled by Tom.

Three Holley 94s sit atop a tri-power manifold on the 1953 Mercury flathead V-8. Mallory provides the spark. An '87 Ford transmission does the gear change duty. The exhaust is handmade; it has cutouts just before the bend under the car. They're loud, too, and the flattie sounds pretty darn healthy through them.

Step inside Tom's coupe and it's like a time warp. Set the "Wayback Machine" for 1956. The dashboard (by Tom) is a modified 1949 Mercury's, but it looks like it was made for the Model A. The steering column is out of a 1956 Ford. There's a "necker's knob" on the white steering wheel and a cigarette pack holder on the passenger door. The upholstery is pure white Naugahyde (stitched by Freddy Hale). The only parts of the interior that aren't white or chrome are the carpets and the pedals. There's even a 1950s pinup air freshener hanging from the mirror, although she lost her scent long ago.

Fifteen-inch chrome wheels are shod with bias-ply whitewall tires, only in a very slight big/little combo. Fronts are 6.70 x 15 and rears are 7.10 x 15.

Tom Culbertson is a founding member of the Road Rockets car club in Indy and his shop is sort of an unofficial clubhouse. See the chapter on Old School Builders for more info on Culbertson's shop.

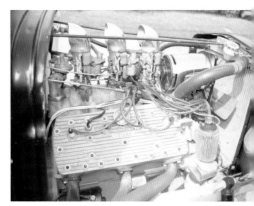

The '53 Merc flathead sounds healthy through cutouts.

Grille shell is a narrowed, sectioned Indiana truck grille.

White interior was upholstered by Brian Whiteis.

The Ford truck steering wheel and gearshift (inset).

Buick drums house Ford brakes.

Indiana wants me!

The1930 Ford coupe seems ready to go cruising.

"Louver Lover's" '31—
Mark Richardson's

1931 Ford Coupe

Low dowwwwnnn! That's what Mark Richardson's '31 Ford coupe is. It's way down. As in, he chopped it three inches, channeled it three inches and Z'ed the frame six inches. Oh, but that wasn't enough. No sir, he also put a drilled, four-inch dropped, I-beam front axle in it. *Dis car is in da weeds!* Like a good hot rod should be.

Mark is a carpenter by trade and he lives in beautiful, historic Marietta, Georgia, just a few miles north of Atlanta. He's a member of the Atlanta Road Kings car club and a rodder to the core.

The man likes his louvers, too. There are 193 on the car altogether. The hood has 60 and the trunk lid has another 133. This thing should whistle as it goes down the road!

Most people opt for the ever popular filled '32 Ford grille shells on their hot rods, but Mark chose the Model-A shell instead. It's painted Rustoleum rattle-can flat black, just like the rest of the car. There's a red custom vertical bar grille in the shell and the Road Kings logo painted in white on the radiator behind it.

Motivation for Mark's ride comes from a 1965 Ford 289 backed by a C4 transmission. The engine's topped off by an Offenhauser manifold and Edelbrock carburetor. It runs an owner-built exhaust system.

Mark Richardson's '31 has been dropped, chopped, and Z'ed. Bright flames stand out over the flat finish.

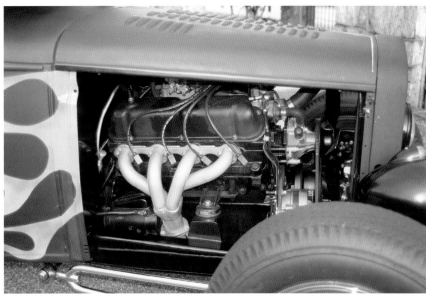

Power comes from a 1965 Ford 289.

Interior boasts a '40 Ford dash with S-W gauges. The black vinyl seats were sewn by Brad Shore

Mr. Richardson also laid-out and painted his own traditional-style flames. In fact, there's not too much on the car that he *didn't* do. He did let a trained professional handle the upholstery duties. Brad Shore sewed the two-inch pleats on the seats.

The interior also features a 1940 Ford dashboard with Stewart-Warner gauges. There's a tilt steering column to make ingress and egress a little more comfortable. The window cranks are from a 1946 Hudson.

The 1935 Ford rear end is blessed with Ford juice brakes. Ford F-1 truck brakes are at the other end. Steel wheels with Ford dog dish caps are wrapped in blackwall bias-ply rubber. Fronts are 5.60-15 and rears are 7.00-15.

Lighting duties are handled by the rodders' favorite—the 1939 Ford taillights and Guide 682-C headlights. It's a popular combo because it's hard to beat.

Mark Richardson's '31 coupe is hard to beat, too, if you're looking for an example of a clean, traditional hot rod Model A.

Ford F-1 truck brakes are on this end.

It's an original 1931 Georgia license plate.

Dixie Fried is the Road Kings' annual rod run.

Road Kings logo is on the radiator and on the plate.

Sixty louvers here...

...133 more here.

CH 25

"Fine Fat-Fendered Ford"— Julie Thomas'

1946 Ford Coupe

The Ford Super Deluxe looks super from the rear as well as the front.

Brad Thomas is a craftsman and he builds some really cool cars. Each one is built to drive, though. Their only trailer time is when they're under construction. After that, if the car goes somewhere, it goes under its own power. This '46 Ford coupe goes under its own power a lot. Other than in foul weather, this is Julie Thomas' daily driver. Most people around their hometown of Columbia, Tennessee, don't even know that she has another car. Wonder what it is?

The '46 Super Deluxe was purchased by Brad and Julie as a restored original, but original cars don't stay that way long in Thommy's Garage. The flathead V-8 and its attendant drivetrain team were yanked out. They are destined for a project to be named later. In their place went a rodders' standby, the venerable 401 Buick Nailhead, backed by a Turbo 400

and a Ford 8-inch with a tall 3.00 to 1 cruising gear. Sanderson headers and dual exhausts give the 401 a mellow sound. Offenhauser finned valve covers dress things up a bit. MSD ignition and a Holley carb on an aluminum manifold complete the engine picture.

As this car was restored already, Brad didn't have to do any bodywork. The shiny black enamel looked fine as delivered. The chrome and stainless trim were already in great shape, too.

The stance is correct for a '46 Ford. Low down.

Halibrands, the rodders' ultimate mag wheel.

The 401 cubic inches of Buick Nailhead will flat move this '46.

There's no doubt what kind of car they're driving!

Safety first for his honey, though, so there's a '37 Ford taillight used as a third brake light. Brilliant!

All the chrome and stainless is as stock as can be.

Speaking of safety, the original Ford brakes were adequate for the power of the flathead V-8, but the extra oomph and weight provided by the Nailhead sent Brad looking for something a little more substantial. The solution turned out to be a Mustang II front end with 11-inch discs. Those are matched to 10-inch Ford drums in the rear. The rear suspension is handled by Posies parallel leaf springs. Wheels are Halibrands all around, 14-inch in front, 15-inch in back. Tires are 195/70 and 235/70, respectively. Julie spends most of her time in the cockpit, so Brad made sure things were comfy in there. Tennessee summers can be brutally hot and humid, so an air conditioning unit hangs beneath the dashboard. There's also a

Pioneer stereo hidden away somewhere so Julie doesn't have to listen to her own singing, or to Brad's when they are traveling to a rod run.

Original style gray cloth is on the seats and door panels. The steering column is an Ididit tilt-style and it's topped with a flat three-spoke steering wheel, sort of an updated sprint car style. AutoMeter gauges reside in an original instrument panel. The Hollywood license topper was a gift from Brad. Julie's coupe was recently used in the filming of a movie on beautiful downtown Columbia's courthouse square.

Spotlight is an early aftermarket accessory.

The interior is comfy, roomy, and traditional.

It's the hot rodder's rake, not the angle that Ford intended.

The 1946 Ford Super Deluxe coupe seems ready to ride into the sunset.

"Hollywood '46" has been filmed in a movie.

The original taillights and fuel door are visible.

A '37 Ford taillight was pressed into service as a third brake light.

So Brad has taken to calling the car Hollywood and bought the topper to drive home his point. The Thomas' Ford may seem a little "street roddy" compared to some of the other cars in this book, and technically, it probably is.

But look at how they handled their transformation and compare it with early hot rodders. The '46 was restored, i.e., like new. They pulled the original engine out and put a powerful V-8 in. Some of the earliest rodders took near-new cars, pulled out the underpowered engine and put in a powerful V-8, be it a Cadillac, Oldsmobile, or the then top-dog, flathead V-8. Brad put modern brakes and better suspension on Julie's '46. Early rodders pulled off the weak mechanical brakes on their Model As and Deuces and used much safer 1940 Ford hydraulic brakes. The comparisons could go on. Julie Thomas' '46 could be considered a current version of a traditional hot rod, while many of the others in this volume are more like replications of early traditional rods. Both are cool, both are traditional.

SECTION 4

Keeping the Flame

CH26

Shops for Your Drop— Old School Builders

The vast majority, a whopping 80 percent of the hot rods featured in this book were built by their owners. That includes either the current owner or a former owner. Not surprisingly, four of those owners are also professional builders, so they build cars for others as well as themselves.

Such talented gents were seemingly more common 40 or 50 years ago; not so much today. American and Western societies have changed vastly in that period of time. Many more people were employed as blue-collar workers in the period spanning the late 1940s through the mid-1960s,

The orange '51 Mercury custom belongs to Back Street Kustoms owner Dave Pareso.

the inarguable heyday of traditional hot rodding. Those were the school days of old school hot rods if such a thing existed.

More people had the skills needed to accomplish hot rod building. Many more of us are desk jockeys or

Back Street Kustoms is a gathering place for local rodders in Colorado Springs.

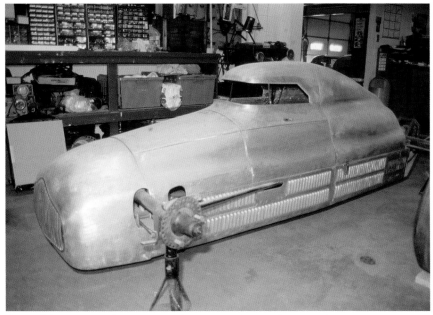
One of the Bonneville racers under restoration at Custom Auto.

no shame in that approach and it can often mean having a finished, drivable hot rod in the garage in a matter of a few months rather than in a few years, if ever.

The problem with that approach is that there simply are not very many bonafide traditional hot rod shops around to choose from. Sure, there are some that call themselves hot rod shops, but the majority of them are really street rod shops.

involved in the service fields these days. Those mechanical skills required for building a hot rod are not a part of our everyday lives anymore. Argue whether this is a good or bad thing, but many people's lives are just more complicated that ever before. It's not uncommon for someone to leave the house at 6 a.m., commute to a job, and not return home until 6 p.m. or later. By the time supper is over, the day is shot and the energy to go out and work in the garage on a hot rod project just is not there.

A Matter of Economics

For some prospective hot rod owners, it makes more sense to have someone else build the car. As a matter of economics, you may be money ahead to work extra hours at your regular job for a given period, and then

invest that money in having a professional do all or part of the work of building your dream hot rod.

If it takes a pro four hours to do a fabrication job that would take you seven, you might be wise to pay him to do it while you get paid to do what *you* are good at. There is certainly

Custom Auto owner Dave Crouse is a knowledgeable, skilled hot rod and race car lover.

Dave Crouse's new Deuce roadster has the Doane Spencer roadster's dash in it.

Others are just parts installation centers, installing bolt-on parts from mail-order companies, often for newer cars, SUVs, and imports; not what we would consider to be hot rods.

Many of the street rod shops do not have the inclination or the skills in-house necessary to build a traditional hot rod. They may build fine street rods, and on the surface it may seem like there wouldn't be much difference in the skills and effort required to build the two, but there certainly is. This is not to say that the good street rod building shops are not skilled, because they are. It's just that it takes some

Lifelong hot rodder Dennis Lesky also has acquired some cool local memorabilia.

different skills and most of all, a different mindset, to build a traditional hot rod.

What to Look For

A *real* hot rod shop (RHRS) will usually be staffed by, and *always* owned by, someone who has a deep respect for the roots of hot rodding. Usually the owner of such a shop will either be someone who has been involved in hot rodding for a very long time, or the descendant of someone like that. There are very few exceptions to

Dennis & Matt Lesky run Ionia Hot Rod Shop and build some great cars for themselves, too.

This is the Nailhead Buick-powered Buick roadster under construction at Ionia Hot Rod.

Culbertson's have developed a twin-tube rod chassis like on this Model A Tudor.

Culbertson's Rod & Custom in Indianapolis is home to long-distance cars like Tom's Lincoln.

that. Unlike the street rod builders on television, he will likely be active in the shop builds, so his hand will be in your hot rod.

There are also very few reasons for that. The average street rod shop owner will consider the amount of effort required to build a traditional rod too time consuming. He would much rather order a chassis from Vendor A with motor mounts already in place, a crate engine from Vendor B, a body from vendor C, grab a selection of billet catalog parts, some seats, stir slowly, bring to a boil, add paint, and *voila*, a finished car. Next please!

Of course it's not quite that simple, nor is there anything wrong with that approach if that's the type of car you want, but you get the idea. Using tried and true suppliers who make their parts

on an assembly line of sorts, even if it's a low volume one, Sammy Street Rod collects his various parts, bolts them together, sends the assembly out the door, and starts all over again.

The RHRS owner, on the other hand, may spend parts of weeks or months helping you to locate the desired 303 Oldsmobile or 392 Hemi engine for your project. Or he may have it sitting in his back room just waiting for a guy like you to come along. He will know where to get the parts to rebuild said engine and he will probably know a reliable mechanic who can do it.

He'll also know how to brace the body on your car so that the car doesn't fold in half when he chops the top three inches. Then he'll know where to make all the

pie cuts to make everything line up again.

He'll be aware of the right period parts to use on what type of car. And the RHRS owner will be able to give you good advice, advice that will make your hot rod dependable and safe to drive. He'll be willing and able to advise you on what not to do, as well as what to do. He will probably become a friend that you can rely on. As a friend, he will also be willing to refuse to do something stupid on your car, no matter how much you think you want it done.

Most rod shops will also work with you on doing the parts of the build that you don't feel qualified to do, or may not have

Tom and Yancey at work on a customer's roadster project.

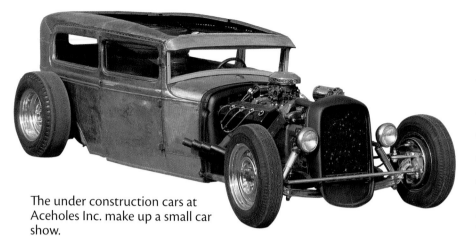

The under construction cars at Aceholes Inc. make up a small car show.

Hot rodders are a pretty accommodating bunch of people. Most guys would be more than willing to show you their car as an example of what your builder-in-waiting can do. They'll tell you what their experience with your builder was like, the highs and the lows. Hopefully the highs will vastly outweigh the lows. Ask them if they know another customer that the builder didn't tell you about who might also have an opinion.

But you're not George Gallup. Eventually you have to stop taking opinion polls and make a decision. When you do, there are some things to keep in mind.

the equipment for. Then you can take the car home and finish it, or at least do the things you feel qualified to do.

Where to Look

So, where does one find such a specialized rod builder? Ask around. People in your part of the country will know who the good guys are. Reputations build slowly and die quickly in this business. The guys who drive the kind of car you want to build will know who can do it. They will also know who cannot, or will not. Ask more than one person, too, because sometimes a personality conflict can cause a good builder to be bad-mouthed by one person and yet be held in high regard by most everyone else.

There is an old adage about walking into an unfamiliar barber shop and trying to decide which barber to use. There are two approaches. One is to ask the guy with the best haircut which one cut his hair, and

then pick that one. The other approach is to just go to the guy with the worst haircut. He didn't cut his own.

When choosing a RHRS, look at the owner's own car. Chances are he built it, so it's a good barometer of what he can do and what his standards are. If it's not up to *your* standards, look elsewhere. Ask for references, too. Check out other cars he has built, especially ones in a similar style to what you are wanting.

Show Me the Money

Count the cost. A reliable, experienced RHRS will be able to give you a reasonably accurate

Bob Merkt uses early '50s dashboards in roadsters for a period look.

estimate of what you dream rod will cost. Keep in mind that it is an estimate and that the price will likely be exceeded by some amount between 10 percent and 20 percent. Until the builder actually gets into your car and sees exactly how much rust repair, and bracing, etc., will be required, he will not know the precise number of hours involved, but he'll be pretty close based on his years of experience.

Expect to pay some money up front and keep paying in regular intervals along the way. In other words, have the coin available and keep it coming. Most RHRS will handle the updates in one of two ways. If your guy is local, he'll probably call on the telephone and tell you that he's to a certain point and ask you to come by and see how the car looks so far. If he's further away, he may call and describe to you where his progress stands, possibly send a few pictures by e-mail, and tell you it's time to pony-up the next check. When the builder sends you an update or calls you and says it's time for another installment, get it to him right away.

Such promptness accomplishes a couple of things for you. One, it keeps your project moving. Most builders will have more than one project underway at a time. This allows them to keep working (and

making money) most hours of the day. They can jump back and forth between projects as they wait for a part to arrive or for a subcontractor to finish his little component. They will *not* want to have to stop on your car because you haven't sent the next check. Their shop space is valuable and

they are not willing to devote any of it to a stalled project. Once a car-in-progress gets pushed to the back corner, it loses its urgency.

Two, it keeps your builder happy and motivated. A happy builder is more likely to go the

The line-up of cars in the works and yet to be started at Aceholes Inc.

extra mile for you. He'll make the extra effort to find the exact part for your car rather than settle for one that's almost but not quite. He'll probably wind up doing a little bonus touch for free. He might be willing to stay an extra 45 minutes to finish a certain job rather than stop at exactly five o'clock and pick up again tomorrow.

Do yourself and your build shop a favor. Have the money available and pay on time. Almost every professional builder I know has told me tales about projects that got stalled or halted because the car's owner didn't have enough money to pay for the work he contracted for. None of those stories was told with a smile.

Kumbaya

The rod builder you choose is on your side. You are a team. The whole project is a combination of your car, his talent, your money, his experience, your preferences, his knowledge, your taste, his taste.

If there are disagreements, and there may or may not be, always keep in mind that this guy is on your side. Don't burn any bridges. They are difficult to rebuild. It's your money, that's true, but it's his reputation on the line each time a new car goes out the overhead door with his name on it. And be sure, even if his name is not physically written on it, his name is still on it.

Try to resolve any problems as amicably and reasonably as possible. Reputable businessmen stand behind their work. That's how they stay in business. Usually any problem can be worked out if both parties are willing to talk things out.

Remember, though, that you chose that particular RHRS, and you did so because of the reputation of your builder and the quality of the work you saw that he had previously done. That included cars that had *the right look*, ostensibly because of his *eye* for that look.

A certain builder that I know (and who is mentioned later in this chapter) was building a fat-fendered hot rod for a customer. It was a car that most of us would consider to be a traditional hot rod.

Gene McKinney is a hot rod Ford parts man to the core.

One day the customer showed up at the shop with a set of Mercedes Benz headlights. The owner of the *real hot rod shop* asked him what he was going to do with those. The customer said he wanted them put in the fenders of his otherwise traditional car, to which the RHRS owner replied, "Who are you gonna get to put those in? I'm not gonna do it."

To this builder, the purity of design on the car he was building, and which everyone would *know* he built, was more important than the risk of upsetting the customer. The builder's reputation is always on the line. Listen to his advice.

Some Real Hot Rod Shops

I'm going to go out on a limb here and recommend some excellent hot rod shops. Technically, I'm not really going out on a limb, because these are all excellent, reliable, reputable hot rod shops.

Allow me to quote myself from earlier in this chapter – "A *real* hot rod shop (RHRS) will usually be staffed, and *always* owned, by someone who has a deep respect for the roots of hot rodding. Usually the owner of such a shop will either be someone who has been involved in hot rodding for a very long time, or the descendant of someone like that."

All 12 of these shops fit those criteria. I know all of these builders personally. One has built a car for me. I have seen inside all of their shops, some even when they weren't expecting me to. I have closely examined finished cars they have built and ones under construction. I have ridden in their cars and have driven some of them. So now I guess I'm staking *my* reputation. These guys are good and I would not hesitate to have any one of them build me a hot rod. In no particular order, here are 12 excellent shops.

West

Back Street Kustoms is a hot rodders' hangout. When Roger Jetter and I went down to Colorado Springs to shoot some of the cars featured in this book, we met the guys at Back Street Kustoms. We didn't have to tell anyone where it was, either. They all knew because they had been there before.

Shop owner Dave Pareso has been active in the Colorado Springs hot rod and custom car scene for more years than he can remember. He has several projects of his own and others under way. Dave personally owns a slick orange custom 1951 Mercury and one of the world's coolest shop trucks, a hot rodded chopped purple Studebaker with Chrysler fins and a custom grille stuffed full of '57 Chevy hood rockets. It was sitting on the chassis dyno when I got there.

Up the road, in Loveland, Colorado, sits one of the best-kept secrets outside Colorado, or at least outside the west. Dave Crouse's **Custom Auto** has to be seen to be believed. Not that there's anything special about the building itself. It's what goes on inside there that will have the red-blooded American (or foreign) hot rodder drooling.

One of Custom Auto's specialties has become restoring old race cars, specifically land speed cars. Dave had a Bonneville

Just one of many projects under way at Gene's is this '34 sedan.

streamliner in the shop under reconstruction the day that I was there. He has also restored the Bell Engine Crankshaft #303 Special and the Berardini Bros. #404 car, among others. His personal AA/FD rail is awaiting restoration.

His hot rods are absolutely beautiful. Roger and I were treated to a tour of Dave's home garage before we went to the shop. There I personally fell head over heels in love with the most beautiful black '32 Ford sedan I have ever seen.

Gene Winfield is a household name in custom car circles. What has been lost on many over the years is that Gene is also a hot rodder. Not only has he built several rods, he has raced at Bonneville and has even recreated his "Thing" Model T coupe that he raced many years ago. The last time I visited his shop he was refurbishing a Deuce roadster that he had built in the 1950s.

Winfield's Custom Shop is located in the desert town of Mojave, California. He's somewhat handy to Bakersfield and Los Angeles, but many people find it worthwhile to ship cars hundreds or even thousands of miles just to have Gene chop their tops. He is known as the master of the 1949 to '51 Mercury chops. He also has created molds to make entire Mercury and 1946 to '48 bodies, as well as Carson-style tops.

Speaking of chopped Mercs, another shop well known for its customs, but equally adept at building hot rods is **Bo Huff's Customs** in East Carbon, Utah. Bo's Bat Outta Utah '32 roadster is about as cool a Deuce as you'll see anywhere. It has been featured in several magazines as have his Mercury and Shoebox Ford customs.

Midwest

Michigan is HQ for the American automotive business and it is chock full of hot rodders. The Detroit Autorama is one of the premier hot rod shows in the world and it attracts some top-notch talent. One such talented builder is Jackson, Michigan's Larry Jordon, owner of **Larry Jordon Enterprises**, and winner of the highly coveted Meguiar's Preservation Award at the 2005 Autorama. That winning car is the Golden Nugget. (See chapter 7).

Larry is a traditionalist and a perfectionist. When I was at his shop to shoot the Nugget, he was working on a custom 1949 or so Oldsmobile. He had taken a coupe and was making a working convertible out of it. If he hadn't told me it was originally a coupe, I wouldn't have been able to tell. The car was braced and finished expertly.

A few miles west of Detroit is the small city of Ionia, Michigan. It's home to the **Ionia Hot Rod Shop**, where the father and son team of Dennis and Matt Lesky crank out some of Michigan's coolest hot rods. Dennis is a retired skilled tradesman from one of the auto plants in Detroit and he has carried those skills over into his hot rod business. When I visited the shop, both he and Matt had some cool projects underway, including a roadster pickup powered by a 389 Pontiac engine.

The showroom at Joe Smith Ford is a great place to hang around in itself.

"Hot rod" is spoken there and Dennis is the owner of the '32 sedan featured in chapter 5. Matt is definitely a chip off the ol' block. His low Nailhead-powered Buick hot rod is going to be very cool indeed.

It stands to reason that the Motor Racing Capital of the World, that's Indianapolis to those not in the know, would have some top hot rod builders. It does not disappoint.

One of the foremost of those is Tom **Culbertson's Rod & Custom** shop. Tom builds cars that are known to be drivers. In fact, his own cars and some other local ones that he built are common fixtures every year at the Viva Las Vegas run in Nevada. They are driven there. So you won't have to look it up, that's 3,700 miles round trip.

Building professionally since 1965, Culbertson specializes in fabrication, customs (his gold '56 Lincoln custom has been in many magazines), and hot rods (see chapter 23). His shop has developed a dual rail frame that is extremely stout, yet relatively light. It can be made in any width and can accommodate any engine and transmission combination. They can use it as the basis for a hot rod or utilize a new or old standard frame, your choice.

Master metalworker Jackie Howerton (see chapter 15) has been crafting hot rods and race

Joe Smith Ford can build any age hot rod you want.

cars for decades. He has restored Indianapolis 500 and USAC Sprint and Champ cars, and is known as one of the premier automotive metalsmiths in the Midwest. The man has even built an entire Indy 500 car.

His **Howerton Racing Products** is located on Gasoline Alley in Indianapolis. They are well-known race car exhaust fabricators for NASCAR and Indy

This is just one barrel full of old Ford axles at Joe Smith's.

cars, but Jackie builds hot rods at his home shop. His own personal builds include a '32 coupe and a high-tech roadster pickup. He always has some sort of top-secret build going, too.

Not far from Indianapolis is Anderson, Indiana, the home of Dave Kinnaman and his one-man shop, **Kinnaman's Kustom Kars.** Dave Kinnaman has been building hot rods and customs for as long as anyone around there can remember. Dave is one of those guys who can look at a fabrication need that has others scratching their heads, and before they can figure out *how* to do it, he has already done it and moved on to the next task.

Dave built a car for me once, a 1936 Pontiac coupe. He ran it back and forth between my garage and his shop a few times, too. He would do what I didn't have the tools or skills to do, then I would work on it at home for a little while, then he would take over again. Dave is extremely talented and also very humble and down-to-earth. He has a keen eye for what looks right, and strong opinions on what would look wrong.

One of the younger pro builders around is Bob Merkt, proprietor of **Aceholes, Inc.,** Delafield, Wisconsin. Bob (also known as Bob Bleed due to his participation in a rock and roll band, Bleed) is the owner and rebuilder of the family heirloom Deuce roadster in chapter 10. He comes from a long line of hot rodders, going all the way back to his grandfather.

Merkt's shop has become a Wisconsin headquarters for what some would term "rat rods." He builds them safe and reliable, though. A more accurate term for some of his builds might be "under-finished traditional rods." His shop was formerly known as Merkt Auto Body, so he has the skills to finish the car out in any way the customer wants, rough or slick. He always has some cool cars under construction in his shop and has a few projects-to-be waiting in the back lot, too.

Southeast

Gene McKinney is the man on the scene at **Gene's Hot Rod Parts** in Riceville, Tennessee, which is about 35 miles north of Chattanooga. Gene is another one of those guys who has been building hot rods since Moses was treading water in the Nile. He's owned his shop and store for over 25 years. Gene's specialty is pre-1940 Ford hot rods. He has a trove of vintage hot rod equipment on hand and has driven a car from Tennessee to Bonneville, raced it, and driven it home. In other words, he's hardcore.

Gene has done much of the work on John McMahan's '39 sedan. (See chapter 14.) His own red '34 coupe is pretty sweet, too. On my last visit to Gene's shop, I saw a couple of early Cadillac V8s waiting in the wings for projects to be named, and a bunch of Ford four cylinder speed equipment.

Joe Smith Ford & Hot Rod Parts in Marietta, Georgia, is a pretty well-known shop, at least in the Southeast. Joe sold the shop several years ago and sort of retired. Chopper builder extraordinaire Hank Young had his shop there in conjunction with the rod and Ford parts business for awhile. Now the shop is owned by Jerry Wilson and Josh Mills. Josh worked with Hank and stayed at the place when Hank struck out to deal in motorcycles exclusively.

Josh's '33 Ford pickup is featured in chapter 20 of this book. Josh is a traditional rod builder exclusively. He builds cars that look like they could have been built forty or fifty years ago. His own truck is his daily driver and he builds customers' vehicles to the same standard.

There you have it, a listing of twelve excellent hot rod shops, world-class in modern manufacturing lingo. By no means are these the only good shops around. They just happen to be ones that I am familiar with. Do some asking around in your own hot rod neighborhood. Or call one of these guys. Happy hot rodding!

CH 27

Sources and Resources—

Shops, Suppliers and Suggested Reading

Hot Rod Builders

Aceholes Inc.
Delafield, WI
262-968-3100
Bob Merkt

Back Street Customs
Colorado Springs, CO
719-577-9577
Dave Pareso

Culbertson's Rod & Custom
Indianapolis, IN
317-244-8271
Tom Culbertson

Custom Auto
Loveland, CO
970-669-6691
Dave Crouse

Gene's Hot Rod Parts
Riceville, TN
423-745-5477
Gene McKinney

Howerton Racing Products
Indianapolis, IN
317-241-0868
Jackie Howerton

Ionia Hot Rod Shop
Ionia, MI
616-527-6051
Dennis & Matt Lesky

Joe Smith Ford & Hot Rod
Marietta, GA
770-426-9850
Josh Mills

Kinnaman's Kustom Kars
Anderson, IN
765-378-5555
Dave Kinnaman

Larry Jordon Enterprises
Jackson,MI
517-536-8455
Larry Jordon

Hot Rod Parts

Egge Machine Company
Santa Fe Springs, CA
562-945-3419
www.egge.com

Honest Charley Speed Shop
Chattanooga, TN
888-795-7077
www.honestcharley.com

Hot Rod & Custom Supply
Plainwell, MI
269-664-3506
www.rodncustom.com

Kanter Auto Products
Boonton, NJ
973-334-9575
www.kanter.com

Night Prowlers
Lamar, MO 64759
417-682-3685
www.thenightprowlers.com

Streamline Hot Rod Parts
Denver, CO
303-623-5789
www.streamlinerods.com

Speedway Motors
Lincoln, NE 68501
402-323-3200
www.speedwaymotors.com

EZ Boy Rod Interiors
Newburyport, MA
866-463-6439
www.rodinteriors.com

O'Brien Truckers
Charlton, MA
508-248-1555
www.obrientruckers.com

Suggested Reading

There are a few excellent books and magazines useful to those interested in traditional or old school hot rods. Here are some suggestions.

Books

Standard Catalog of V-8 Engines, John Gunnell, Krause Publications

Hot Rod Milestones, Ken Gross & Robert Genat, Car Tech Books

The All-American Hot Rod, Michael Dregni, Editor, Voyageur Press

Ford Hot Rods, Dain Gingerelli, MBI Books

The Birth of Hot Rodding, Robert Genat & Don Cox, MBI Books

California Hot Rodder, Jay Carnine, Graffiti Publications

Bangin' Gears & Bustin' Heads, Roger Jetter, Publish America

Hot Rodder, Albert Drake, Flat Out Press

Flat Out, Albert Drake, Flat Out Press

Souping the Stock Engine, Roger Huntington, Fisher Books

Periodicals

Ol' Skool Rodz Magazine (bi-monthly)

Car Kulture DeLuxe Magazine (bi-monthly)

Hop Up Magazine (annually)

Rod & Custom Magazine (monthly)

The Rodders Journal (quarterly)

Traditional Rod & Kulture Magazine (quarterly)